Women
of the
Bible

Stick with boring.

For Circle 6 study
Fall & Winter 2024

iders

Table of Contents

Foreword

I lead a ladies' Bible study at Abundant Life Community Church in Grass Valley, California. While attempting to choose a new study, several women asked if we could learn about the lives of Bible women. We researched available books, but none seemed in-depth enough or in usable format for our group. Knowing I have written several books, they asked me if I would write the curriculum for them. It has been a joy to do that.

Their next request was to get it published so they could keep the material and so that other women could benefit from it. So here it is. I thank each of these Bible students for their help in testing and editing the material. I hope it blesses the hearts of other students of God's word.

Acknowledgements

Thanks to all the patient ladies in our study who offered constructive comments and asked the right questions, enabling me to write this tribute to God's women.

Eve: _____

Just Imagine

Think what it must have been like to be Eve. Start with her "awakening" at her creation from Adam's rib.

Read All About Eve:

Genesis 2:18) And the Lord God said, "It is not good that man should be alone; I will make him a helper comparable to him."

19) Out of the ground the Lord God formed every beast of the field and every bird of the air, and brought them to Adam to see what he would call them. And whatever Adam called each living creature, that was its name. 20) So Adam gave names to all cattle, to the birds of the air, and to every beast of the field. But for Adam there was not found a helper comparable to him. 21) And the Lord God caused a deep sleep to fall on Adam, and he slept; and He took one of his ribs, and closed up the flesh in its place. 22) Then the rib which the Lord God had taken from man He made into a woman, and He brought her to the man.

23) And Adam said,

> *"This is now bone of my bones*
> *And flesh of my flesh;*
> *She shall be called Woman,*
> *Because she was taken out of Man."*

24) Therefore a man shall leave his father and mother and be joined to his wife, and they shall become one flesh. 25) And they were both naked, the man and his wife, and were not ashamed.

Genesis 3:1) Now the serpent was more cunning than any beast of the field which the Lord God had made. And he said to the woman, "Has God indeed said, 'You shall not eat of every tree of the garden'?"

2) And the woman said to the serpent, "We may eat the fruit of the trees of the garden; 3) "but of the fruit of the tree which is in the midst of the garden, God has said, 'You shall not eat it, nor shall you touch it, lest you die."

4) Then the serpent said to the woman, "You shall not surely die, 5) "For God knows that in the day you eat of it your eyes will be opened, and you will be like God, knowing good and evil."

6) So when the woman saw that the tree was good for food, that it was pleasant to the eyes, and a tree desirable to make one wise, she took of its fruit and ate. She also gave to her husband with her, and he ate. 7) Then the eyes of both of them were opened, and they knew that they were naked; and they sewed fig leaves together and made themselves coverings.

8) And they heard the sound of the Lord God walking in the garden in the cool of the day, and Adam and his wife hid themselves from the presence of the Lord God among the trees of the garden.

9) Then the Lord God called to Adam and said to him, "Where are you?"

10) So he said, "I heard Your voice in the garden, and I was afraid because I was naked; and I hid myself."

11) And He said, "Who told you that you were naked? Have you eaten from the tree of which I commanded you that you should not eat?"

12) Then the man said, "The woman whom You gave to be with me, she gave me of the tree, and I ate."

13) And the Lord God said to the woman, "What is this you have done?"

The woman said, "The serpent deceived me, and I ate."

14) So the Lord God said to the serpent:
"Because you have done this,
You are cursed more than all cattle,
And more than every beast of the field;
On your belly you shall go,
And you shall eat dust
All the days of your life.
15) And I will put enmity
Between you and the woman,
And between your seed and her Seed;
He shall bruise your head,
And you shall bruise His heel."

16) To the woman He said:
"I will greatly multiply your sorrow and your conception;
In pain you shall bring forth children;
Your desire shall be for your husband,

And he shall rule over you."

17) Then to Adam He said, "Because you have heeded the voice of your wife, and have eaten from the tree of which I commanded you, saying, 'You shall not eat of it':
"Cursed is the ground for your sake;
In toil you shall eat of it
All the days of your life.
18) Both thorns and thistles it shall bring forth for you,
And you shall eat the herb of the field.
19) In the sweat of your face you shall eat bread
Till you return to the ground,
For out of it you were taken;
For dust you are,
And to dust you shall return."

20) And Adam called his wife's name Eve, because she was the mother of all living. 21) Also for Adam and his wife the Lord God made tunics of skin, and clothed them.

22) Then the Lord God said, "Behold, the man has become like one of Us, to know good and evil. And now, lest he put out his hand and take also of the tree of life, and eat, and live forever"— 23) therefore the Lord God sent him out of the garden of Eden to till the ground from which he was taken. 24) So He drove out the man; and He placed cherubim at the east of the garden of Eden, and a flaming sword which turned every way, to guard the way to the tree of life.

Any questions?

Clarifications:

Her names:
woman – kind of a generic; actually means man-ess.

Adam – like Mrs. Adam; speaking of an indissoluble unity.

Eve – given by Adam; response to God's prophecy that through her seed the giver of eternal life would come.

Chapter 1 summarizes Adam and Eve's creation. Chapter 2 gives the details.

2:23 – **Adam's statement** at her creation: "Wow!"

Let's think about it.

1. What significance might there be to God using Adam's rib to form her?

2. Why was she created?

3. List all the firsts that you can think of that Eve experienced:

4. What does the Bible tell us about Eve's world? (Genesis 2)

5. Why do you think she fell for Satan's trick?

6. 1 John 2:16 describes sin. Relate it to Eve's temptation. Does Satan use any other approaches?

7. How did Eve misquote God's command? (Genesis 2:16-17 and 3:2-3.)

8. Where was Adam during the temptation? (vs. 3:6)

9. What changed when they disobeyed God?

10. Relate the Bible story to the Pandora myth. Where do you think that story came from? Which came first? Why?

11. Read 1 Corinthians 15:21-22, 2 Corinthians 11:3, and 1 Timothy 2:11-15. Why is Adam held responsible for Eve's sin? What consequences does Adam suffer? Eve? What consequences fall on their progeny?

12. What is the significance of God's provision of clothing made from animal skins? (3:21)

13. Why didn't God want them to remain in the garden? (3:22-24)

The rest of the story:

So God listened to Adam and Eve's blame game and pronounced judgment on each of them and on the serpent. The first time we read about the Messiah is in the phrase "Seed of the woman." Apparently God did not explain further, so we can infer from Eve's response to the birth of her first child: "I have gotten a man (maybe even THE man) from the Lord." She may have thought the fulfillment of God's promise was already provided.

Now skip ahead a few years. Eve has borne a second child. Obviously the first parents taught their sons about God, even though they no longer had a face-to-face relationship with Him. When God provided those first garments, He must have demonstrated to them the ritual of animal sacrifice, a picture of the Redeemer's future death for the sins of the world. Worship included death.

So we have the grown-up sons of Adam and Eve. They came to worship the God of their parents. Did they understand God's requirements?

Each son brought an offering from his work. It is often suggested that Cain was a farmer (plant products) and Abel a herdsman. The Bible doesn't indicate this. We can assume both men had equal access to plants and animals. After all, at that time there was only one family on earth. For whatever reason, Cain brought an offering of plants and Abel an offering of animals. Plants do not have blood to shed, so they do not picture the death of the Messiah. For that reason Cain's worship was rejected.

But look! God gave Cain a second chance. He could still have brought an animal offering. Instead, he ignored God's offer, became angry and bitter, and murdered his brother.

Imagine Eve's remorse. The very child she thought was God's prophecy committed the most horrendous sin. She was left without children. The younger was dead and the older was banished. Surely she blamed herself for bringing sin into the world.

God didn't leave her childless. Eventually (130 years later) another child was born to her: Seth. He seems to have become a godly man. And numerous other children were born to her in the long life that she and Adam had together after Seth's birth.

What's in it for me?

1. In what ways are you like Eve?

2. How are you different from Eve?

3. Did God remain active in their lives after they left the garden? How do you know?

4. Do you know someone (or yourself) whose behavior drove her away from God but God pursued her anyway?

5. Why do you think God related this story in the Bible?

6. Fill in an appropriate title for this lesson.

7. What do you personally take away from Eve for your own life?

Application:

I'm not perfect. Even the first woman was not perfect. She sinned and got us all into trouble. I could say it would have been different if it had been me in the garden instead of Eve, but I would have failed just as she did. However, God showed His grace to Eve and He shows it to me. As His child, I need to show that grace to the people in my life – and to myself.

Response:

Has God touched your heart or taught you something new as you have studied about Eve? Write your prayer of response to Him.

For Further Study:
Genesis 1:26-28; 2:8-5:5; 2 Corinthians 11:3; 1 Timothy 2:11-15

Sarah: _____

Just Imagine:

These are the facts that we know about Sarah: Born in Ur; married to half-brother Abram who is 10 years her senior; moves to Haran; at age 65 begins nomadic life moving to Canaan; shortly after moves to Egypt because of famine; expelled from Egypt, back to Canaan with new maid; 76 when Ishmael is born; 90 when Isaac is born; dies at 127.

From what you know of Sarah, relate her life to your present age. If you were Sarah, what do you think you would be doing, thinking, and planning right now?

Read About Sarah:

Genesis 12:1) Now the Lord had said to Abram:
    "Get out of your country,
    From your family
    And from your father's house,
    To a land that I will show you.
    2) I will make you a great nation;
    I will bless you
    And make your name great;
    And you shall be a blessing.
    3) I will bless those who bless you,
    And I will curse him who curses you;
    And in you all the families of the earth shall be blessed."

4) So Abram departed as the Lord had spoken to him, and Lot went with him. And Abram was seventy-five years old when he departed from Haran.

5) Then Abram took Sarai his wife and Lot his brother's son, and all their possessions that they had gathered, and the people whom they had acquired in Haran, and they departed to go to the land of Canaan. So they came to the land of Canaan.

Genesis 12:10) Now there was a famine in the land, and Abram went down to Egypt to dwell there, for the famine was severe in the land. 11) And it came to pass, when he was close to entering Egypt, that he said to Sarai his wife, "Indeed I know that you are a woman of beautiful countenance. 12) Therefore it will happen, when the Egyptians see you, that they will say, 'This is his wife'; and they will kill me but they will let you live. 13) Please say you are my sister, that it may be well with me for your sake, and that I may live because of you."

14) So it was, when Abram came into Egypt, that the Egyptians saw the woman, that she was very beautiful. 15) The princes of Pharaoh also saw her and commended her to Pharaoh. And the woman was taken to Pharaoh's house. 16) He treated Abram well for her sake. He had sheep, oxen, male donkeys, male and female servants, female donkeys, and camels.

17) But the Lord plagued Pharaoh and his house with great plagues because of Sarai, Abram's wife. 18) And Pharaoh called Abram and said, "What is this you have done to me? Why did you not tell me that she was your wife? 19) Why did you say, 'She is my sister'? I might have taken her as my wife. Now therefore, here is your wife; take her and go your way."

20) So Pharaoh commanded his men concerning him; and they sent him away, with his wife and all that he had.

Genesis 13:1) Then Abram went up from Egypt, he and his wife and all that he had, and Lot with him, to the South.

Genesis 16:1) Now Sarai, Abram's wife, had borne him no children. And she had an Egyptian maidservant whose name was Hagar. 2) So Sarai said to Abram, "See now, the Lord has restrained me from bearing children. Please, go in to my maid; perhaps I shall obtain children by her."

And Abram heeded the voice of Sarai. 3) Then Sarai, Abram's wife, took Hagar her maid, the Egyptian, and gave her to her husband Abram to be his wife, after Abram had dwelt ten years in the land of Canaan. 4) So he went in to Hagar, and she conceived. And when she saw that she had conceived, her mistress became despised in her eyes.

5) Then Sarai said to Abram, "My wrong be upon you! I gave my maid into your embrace; and when she saw that she had conceived, I became despised in her eyes. The Lord judge between you and me."

6) So Abram said to Sarai, "Indeed your maid is in your hand; do to her as you please."

7) And when Sarai dealt harshly with her, she fled from her presence.

Genesis 17:15) Then God said to Abraham, "As for Sarai your wife, you shall not call her name Sarai, but Sarah shall be her name. 16) "And I will bless her and also give you a son by her; then I will bless her, and she shall be a mother of nations; kings of peoples shall be from her."

Any questions?

Clarifications:

Abram – exalted father

Abraham – father of a multitude

Sarai – contentious?

Sarah – princess

Intermarriage in families was frequent in the early years. Being closer to the time of creation the line had not mutated to cause the birth defects now exhibited by close marriages. Unions joined cousins and half-siblings, as in the case of Abraham and Sarah.

Heirs could be borne of concubines, particularly if the child was received in the lap of the barren wife.

A **childless** man usually gave his inheritance to the overseer of his holdings: in Abraham's case, that would have been Eliezer of Damascus.

Let's Think About It:

1. Even as a nomad, Abram was known as a rich man. What do you think Sarah's life was like back in Ur?

2. Exactly who did God call? (Genesis 11:31; 12:1-4)

3. Genesis 12:1-3 is known as the Abrahamic Covenant. Who is it between?

4. What did it promise?

5. What were the conditions?

6. The call was to go to Canaan, but Terah led his family only part way – to Haran. It wasn't until Terah died that Abram led his family on to Canaan. They were in Canaan a short time when what happened? (Genesis 12:10-20)

7. How did they respond?

8. How did Abram, known as the man of faith, respond to his fears about Egypt?

9. How do you think Sarai felt about that?

10. How did God protect Sarai?

11. List some results of their stay in Egypt?

The Rest of the Story:

Life went on in the tents. Abram and Sarai approached the century mark, although she kept her youthful beauty. Imagine their confusion about the son God promised them.

When Ishmael was thirteen years old, God appeared to Abram again and repeated the covenant. Abram fell on his face in worship. God confirmed the covenant by telling Abram He had changed their names: from Abram (exalted father) to Abraham (father of a multitude) and Sarai (princely) to Sarah (ruler).

God was finally moving. Shortly after that visit, the Lord God and two "men" visited their encampment. In customary desert host fashion, Abraham scurried around to provide a sumptuous meal and he ordered Sarah to make bread. When they finally sat down to the meal, the Lord asked where Sarah was. Of course, He knew she was eavesdropping in the next tent. He then announced to

Abraham that Sarah would bear him the promised child within the year.

Sarah laughed. And who could blame her? She would be 90 years old when the child was born. She knew the reproductive part of her body had long ceased to function. The Lord's announcement was impossible.

The Lord admonished Sarah for her laugh of disbelief. She still had much to learn about our miracle working God.

Even in this last year of waiting for God's miracle, once again Abram lacked faith in God's protection and asked Sarai to lie about their relationship. Once again God protected her and allowed Abraham to be humiliated among his neighbors.

The long awaited day finally came, and 90-year-old Sarah gave birth to Isaac, whose very name means Laughter. He was her delight and she continued to develop her trust in God because of him.

What's in it for me?

1. What trust issues are you still working on?

2. What miracles have you seen in your life to help you trust Him?

3. What was Sarah's relationship with Abraham like? (1 Peter 3:5-7)

4. Discuss Sarah's spiritual significance. (Galatians 4:21-31)

6. What do you personally take away from Sarah for your own life?

5. Fill in an appropriate title for this lesson.

Application:

We do not deal with perfect people. Sarah followed
Abraham's orders, even though she must have feared to do
so and even felt hurt and angry at his request. But God
protected her. I can trust God to protect me and grow my
faith in all circumstances. I can exhibit this grace to family,
friends and neighbors to give them that same hope.

Response:

Has God touched your heart or taught you something new
in this study of Sarah? Write your prayer of response to
Him.

For Further Study:
Genesis 11:27–18:15; 20:1–21:21; 22:1–23:20; Hebrews
11:8-12; 1 Peter 3:5-7

Rebekah:_____

Just Imagine:

You are a teen girl in Bible times, living a protected life in an idolatrous society. What are your dreams? Your household chores include kitchen duty, which involves trips to the city well. What are your thoughts when you find a wealthy stranger at the well?

Read All About Rebekah:

Genesis 24:9) So the servant put his hand under the thigh of Abraham his master, and swore to him concerning this matter.

10) Then the servant took ten of his master's camels and departed, for all his master's goods were in his hand. And he arose and went to Mesopotamia, to the city of Nahor. 11) And he made his camels kneel down outside the city by

*a well of water at evening time, the time when women go
out to draw water.*

*12) Then he said, "O Lord God of my master Abraham,
please give me success this day, and show kindness to my
master Abraham. 13) Behold, here I stand by the well of
water, and the daughters of the men of the city are coming
out to draw water. 14) "Now let it be that the young woman
to whom I say, 'Please let down your pitcher that I may
drink,' and she says, 'Drink, and I will also give your
camels a drink – let her be the one You have appointed for
Your servant Isaac. And by this I will know that You have
shown kindness to my master."*

*15) And it happened, before he had finished speaking, that
behold, Rebekah, ... came out with her pitcher on her
shoulder. 16) Now the young woman was very beautiful to
behold, a virgin; no man had known her. And she went
down to the well, filled her pitcher, and came up.*

*17) And the servant ran to meet her and said, "Please let
me drink a little water from your pitcher."*

18) So she said, "Drink, my lord."

*Then she quickly let her pitcher down to her hand, and
gave him a drink. 19) And when she had finished giving
him a drink, she said, "I will draw water for your camels
also, until they have finished drinking."*

*20) Then she quickly emptied her pitcher into the trough,
ran back to the well to draw water, and drew for all his*

camels. 21) And the man, wondering at her, remained silent so as to know whether the Lord had made his journey prosperous or not.

22) So it was, when the camels had finished drinking, that the man took a golden nose ring weighing half a shekel, and two bracelets for her wrists weighing ten shekels of gold, 23) and said, "Whose daughter are you? Tell me, please, is there room in your father's house for us to lodge?"

24) So she said to him, "I am the daughter of Bethuel, Milcah's son, whom she bore to Nahor."

25) Moreover she said to him, "We have both straw and feed enough, and room to lodge."

26) Then the man bowed down his head and worshiped the Lord. 27) And he said, "Blessed be the Lord God of my master Abraham, who has not forsaken His mercy and His truth toward my master. As for me, being on the way, the Lord led me to the house of my master's brethren."

28) So the young woman ran and told her mother's household these things.

Genesis 24:49) "Now if you will deal kindly and truly with my master, tell me. And if not, tell me, that I may turn to the right hand or to the left."

50) Then Laban and Bethuel answered and said, "The thing comes from the Lord; we cannot speak to you either

bad or good. 51) Here is Rebekah before you; take her and go, and let her be your master's son's wife, as the Lord has spoken."

Genesis 24:58) Then they called Rebekah and said to her, "Will you go with this man?"

And she said, "I will go."

59) So they sent away Rebekah their sister and her nurse, and Abraham's servant and his men.

60) And they blessed Rebekah and said to her:
> *"Our sister, may you become*
> *The mother of thousands of ten thousands;*
> *And may your descendants possess*
> *The gates of those who hate them."*

61) Then Rebekah and her maids arose, and they rode on the camels and followed the man. So the servant took Rebekah and departed.

63) Now Isaac went out to meditate in the field in the evening; and he lifted his eyes and looked, and there, the camels were coming. Then Rebekah lifted her eyes, and when she saw Isaac she dismounted from her camel; 65) for she had said to the servant, "Who is this man walking in the field to meet us?"

The servant said, "It is my master."

So she took a veil and covered herself.

66) And the servant told Isaac all the things that he had done. 67) Then Isaac brought her into his mother Sarah's tent; and he took Rebekah and she became his wife, and he loved her. So Isaac was comforted after his mother's death.

Any questions?

Clarifications:

Rebekah – means captivating

Placing the hand under the thigh – kind of like a lie detector test

Isaac and Rebekah: a love story – almost like a fairy tale

New Testament truth: the Father (God) sent His servant (Holy Spirit) into the world to get a bride (believers) for His Son (Jesus Christ)

Let's Think About It.

1. What do you know about Isaac? Describe him.

2. What do you know about Rebekah? Describe her.

3. Why do you think Rebekah was willing to go with the servant to become Isaac's bride?

4. Describe how the marriage between Isaac and Rebekah developed.

5. Compare Genesis 24:3 with 2 Corinthians 6:14. How does this explain Abraham's directive to his servant?

6. What can we conclude from this about Rebekah's family's spiritual life?

7. What place does prayer have in the story?

The Rest of the Story:

We don't know how old Rebekah was when she married, but probably not out of her teens. We do know Isaac was 40 (Genesis 25:20). That would be a scandalous difference today – not so in their day.

However, once again the wife seemed to be barren, for 20 years went by before Isaac pleaded with God to send them children.

God answered by sending fraternal twins: two sons who looked and acted totally opposite. Even before their birth they struggled for dominance in the womb – to the point that Rebekah asked God what was going on. (Genesis 25:22)

God told her she was carrying two nations who would continue to fight, and that the older child would serve the younger. We know the story of how Esau was born with Jacob grasping his heel in the delivery. Their names tell part of the story. Esau means "hairy;" Jacob means "supplanter," or "deceitful."

So far they were one happy family. Or were they? As the boys grew, problems developed. Isaac was a mild mannered man, willing to make concessions to the well stealing tribes around him, and following his father's error of lying about his relationship with his wife to save his own skin. As the sons grew, Esau's hunting exploits entertained Isaac, who lusted after the gamy meals Esau brought him.

Rebekah also played a part in this favorites game. She loved the companionship of Jacob, the quiet son who joined her in the kitchen and appreciated the finer things of life. She surely remembered that God had told her Jacob, the younger, would be greater than Esau, the older. She determined her favorite would rule.

Time went on. The boys became men. Esau's rebellious heart led him to despise much of his family's belief system. Once, when he was hungry, he sold Jacob his birthright for a bowl of stew. Being spiritual head of the family meant nothing to him, and he trusted in himself to accumulate his own fortune. Equally telling, he married two Hethite women, who caused grief to his parents.

Rebekah remembered God's pronouncement but, like Sarah before her, she could not wait for God to act. When she heard Isaac tell Esau to bring him a meal from fresh game so that he could give him "the blessing," her devious mind went into gear. As soon as Esau was out of sight, she called Jacob and enlisted him in her plan. While he cooked a goat stew, she used the kid skin to fashion gloves that would deceive Isaac into thinking Jacob's hands were Esau's.

Isaac, at 100 years, could no longer see. They only had to rely on what he heard, smelled, and felt to deceive him.

We know the story. The trick worked. Jacob received Isaac's blessing. Esau was left out. Rebekah and her favorite son triumphed!

Or did they? Jacob had gone too far this time, and Esau threatened to kill him. So Rebekah had to plot further to save her favorite. Feigning concern about his possible marriage to an unbeliever, she got Isaac to send him off with his blessing to Rebekah's brother's house in Padan Aram -- for a "few days," until Esau's anger cooled.

A few days? More than twenty years! When Jacob finally returned, Isaac was still alive and Esau had forgiven him, but Rebekah was dead.

I wonder if she ever took responsibility for the losses in her life. I picture a bitter old woman, estranged from her aged husband, alienated from her oldest son and his godless wives, living only for the day her favorite son returns from exile. A day that never comes.

What's in it for Me?

Wow! What a lot of lessons in Rebekah's life. She started out with so much blessing, but she became impatient waiting for the fulfillment of God's promises. A talented, calculating woman, she used those skills to manipulate

God's plans. A loving woman, she turned that love into idolatry of her favorite son, alienating all others.

1.What do we learn about God's leading? (Psalm 32:8; 143:8)

2.What principles can those who are looking for a life partner learn from this story?

3.What do you personally take away from Rebekah for your own life?

4.Fill in an appropriate title for his lesson.

Application:

God tells it like it was. We don't need to manipulate God.
Our own way looks right to us, but God's way is always
better. I must ask God to help me wait on His answers and
accept them. I need His help to keep me from developing
favorites.

Response:

Has God touched your heart or taught you something new
in this study of Rebekah? Write your prayer of response to
Him.

For Further Study:
Genesis 24:1-67; 25:19-34; 26:1-34; 27:1-46; 28:1-9.

Rachel and Leah:____

Just Imagine

A handsome older man has fallen in love with you. He loves you so much he has worked for your father for seven years for the privilege of marrying you. It's finally your wedding day. You have feasted with the women, laughing and learning about the intimacies of marriage. Night has fallen and you are ready to consummate your marriage. Your father enters the women's quarters. You rise, but he tells you to sit back down. He reminds you of your culture: the younger daughter must not marry before the older daughter. He orders you and Leah to exchange clothing. In a few moments he returns and leads the heavily veiled Leah out to your betrothed husband.

How do you respond?

Now, change to Leah's viewpoint? What are you thinking?

Read About Rachel and Leah:

Genesis 29:9) Now while he was still speaking with them, Rachel came with her father's sheep, for she was a shepherdess. 10) And it came to pass, when Jacob saw Rachel the daughter of Laban his mother's brother, and the sheep of Laban his mother's brother, that Jacob went near and rolled the stone from the well's mouth, and watered the flock of Laban his mother's brother. 11) Then Jacob kissed Rachel, and lifted up his voice and wept.

12) And Jacob told Rachel that he was her father's relative and that he was Rebekah's son. So she ran and told her father.

13) Then it came to pass, when Laban heard the report about Jacob his sister's son, that he ran to meet him, and embraced him and kissed him, and brought him to his house. So he told Laban all these things.

14) And Laban said to him, "Surely you are my bone and my flesh."

And he stayed with him for a month. 15) Then Laban said to Jacob, "Because you are my relative, should you therefore serve me for nothing? Tell me, what should your wages be?"

16) Now Laban had two daughters: the name of the elder was Leah, and the name of the younger was

Rachel. 17) Leah's eyes were delicate, but Rachel was beautiful of form and appearance.

18) Now Jacob loved Rachel; so he said, "I will serve you seven years for Rachel your younger daughter."

19) And Laban said, "It is better that I give her to you than that I should give her to another man. Stay with me."

20) So Jacob served seven years for Rachel, and they seemed only a few days to him because of the love he had for her.

21) Then Jacob said to Laban, "Give me my wife, for my days are fulfilled, that I may go in to her."

22) And Laban gathered together all the men of the place and made a feast. 23) Now it came to pass in the evening, that he took Leah his daughter and brought her to Jacob; and he went in to her. 24) And Laban gave his maid Zilpah to his daughter Leah as a maid.

25) So it came to pass in the morning, that behold, it was Leah.

And he said to Laban, "What is this you have done to me? Was it not for Rachel that I served you? Why then have you deceived me?

26) And Laban said, "It must not be done so in our country, to give the younger before the firstborn. 27)

Fulfill her week, and we will give you this one also for the service which you will serve with me still another seven years."

28) Then Jacob did so and fulfilled her week. So he gave him his daughter Rachel as wife also. 29) And Laban gave his maid Bilhah to his daughter Rachel as a maid. 30) Then Jacob also went in to Rachel, and he also loved Rachel more than Leah. And he served with Laban still another seven years.

Any questions?

Clarifications:

The kiss – they were cousins. He was glad to find family.

"**Fulfill her week.**" Some commentators say that means Jacob had to work another seven years before he could marry Rachel. That doesn't fit the following scripture's time frame. It may mean he could have her immediately if he promised to serve another seven years. It may also mean he needed to celebrate Leah's marriage for a week. Then he could marry Rachel. But he still had to serve another seven years for Rachel.

Let's think about it.

1. Why was Jacob in Haran? What evidence do you find of God's leading? (Genesis 27:42-43; 28:10-22; 29:4-6)

2. As the possessor of the family birthright, Jacob would inherit a double portion of his father's holdings. Read his blessing from Isaac in Genesis 27:27-29. So why is he forced to work for Uncle Laban?

3. Describe Uncle Laban.

Genesis 29:14-15.

Genesis 29:23-27

Genesis 31:4-7

Genesis 31:14-16

4. Describe Rachel.

Genesis 29:16-17, 30-31;

Genesis 30:1-8

5. Describe Leah.

Genesis 29:16-17, 30-35

6. From your knowledge of human nature, what do you imagine Jacob's household was like?

7. There are a lot of negatives in this account. What are some positives?

8.What do you personally take away from studying the lives of Rachel and Leah?

9. Fill in an appropriate title for this chapter.

The rest of the story:

Sibling rivalry. Jealousy. Idolatry. Tricky business dealings. Stealing. Deceit. Life in Rachel and Leah's time was not much different from today.

Rachel got her man. Imagine the love of a man willing to work seven years to gain a wife! The Bible says those years seemed like only a few days because of the love he had for her. Is there a more romantic statement in Scripture?

All that time Leah looked on, longing for someone to love her like that. Hopeless – and then – Laban gave her to the man she secretly loved. Did she fear her sister's wrath? Surely she knew this was not going to be one happy family. She approached her marriage with mixed emotions, both elated and terrified to obey her father – but obey she must.

God was in control. Jacob loved Rachel best, but God loved Leah and rewarded her with children. Leah revealed her heart toward God in the names she gave her children: Reuben – the Lord has surely looked on my affliction; Simeon – the Lord has heard; Levi – my husband will be attached to me; Judah – Praise the Lord! Issachar – God has given me my wages; Zebulun – my husband will dwell with me.

It is revealing that although Rachel did ask God for children (Genesis 30:22), she still attacked Jacob, as though it were his fault: "Give me children, or else I die." Jacob's angry retort pointed her to God, but her response was to give Jacob her maid, that she might have surrogate children. Apparently they hadn't learned from Sarah's mistake. It is also ironic that she died during the birth of her second child (Genesis 35:16-20).

What about the religious life of this family? Jacob had an epiphany at Bethel on the way to Haran. Deceptive as he was, he still trusted in the God of Abraham and Isaac. Laban, on the other hand, still kept household idols. Rachel trusted in the good luck those idols were thought to bring, for she stole them from her father when Jacob moved his family back to the promised land. Then she concealed them in a saddle, sat on it, and begged her father's forgiveness for not rising when he searched her tent. She said "… the manner of women is with me," an illusion to her monthly period. Another lie, for she was probably pregnant with Benjamin at the time.

If Jacob had known Rachel kept Laban's household idols he would not have boldly declared that Laban could kill whomever had taken them. He must have heard her story afterward, for as they neared Bethel, he collected and buried all foreign idols and demanded they purify themselves and change their garments in order to worship Jehovah God.

Rachel's crowning achievement was the birth of her two sons. Joseph was a toddler when Rachel died. There is no mention of who cared for Rachel's children, but these last two children of Jacob – Joseph in particular – developed a relationship with God that the older sons did not have. Maybe the return to Bethel and Jacob's commitment to

God made a difference in the way he raised his youngest children.

Rachel died before the family settled back in Canaan. Jacob loved her to the end. With her passing, Leah finally became the number one wife that her father had pushed upon her. The six sons of Leah, two of Rachel's maid, two of Leah's maid, and Rachel's two became the heads of the twelve tribes of Israel. However fractured their household must have been, Rachel and Leah were known as "the two who built the house of Israel." (Ruth 4:11)

What's in it for me?

1. What from this account can I copy in my life?

2. What should I watch out for?

3. What spiritual truth I can rest on?

4.What do you personally take away from Rachel and Leah's story for yourself?

5.Write an appropriate title for this lesson.

Application:

List the principles from Jacob's family that you see applying to life today.

Response:

Has something about Rachel and/or Leah touched your own heart? Is there something you should talk to God about from this study? Take a minute to write your prayer.

For Further Study:
Genesis 28:1-5; 29:1-35:26; Ruth 4:11.

Dinah: _____

Just Imagine

You are the oldest wife of a nomadic chieftain. Your clan has recently moved from the desert town where you were born. As the number one wife, you must supervise the packing and unpacking as well as the day-to-day activities of food preparation and cleaning. You also try to keep peace in your family, which consists of yourself, your younger sister, two female servant/concubines, your six sons, four sons of your husband's concubines, and a toddler son of your sister/co-wife. With so much testosterone in the camp, you hold your daughter Dinah close, savoring all your moments together. She is your husband's only girl child – and maybe a little spoiled because of this.

Your family has set up camp outside a large town. The town's spring festival is in full swing. Fifteen-year-old Dinah is begging for permission to go check out the young urban women. You are concerned. She's never gone anywhere alone before. She doesn't mention checking out the young men, but you know they'll be checking her out.

What are your concerns?

What do you tell Dinah?

Why do you let her go?

Read All About Dinah:

Genesis 34:1) Now Dinah the daughter of Leah, whom she had borne to Jacob, went out to see the daughters of the land. 2) And when Shechem the son of Hamor the Hivite, prince of the country, saw her, he took her and lay with her, and violated her. 3) His soul was strongly attracted to Dinah the daughter of Jacob, and he loved the young woman and spoke kindly to the young woman.

4) So Shechem spoke to his father Hamor, saying, "Get me this young woman as a wife."

5) And Jacob heard that he had defiled Dinah his daughter. Now his sons were with his livestock in the field; so Jacob held his peace until they came.

6) Then Hamor the father of Shechem went out to Jacob to speak with him. 7) And the sons of Jacob came in from the field when they heard it, and the men were grieved and very angry, because he had done a disgraceful thing in Israel by lying with Jacob's daughter, a thing which ought not to be done.

8) But Hamor spoke with them saying, "The soul of my son Shechem longs for your daughter. Please give her to him as a wife. 9) And make marriages with us; give your daughters to us, and take our daughters to yourselves. 10) So you shall dwell with us, and the land shall be before you. Sell and trade in it, and acquire possessions for yourselves in it."

11) Then Shechem said to her father and her brothers, "Let me find favor in your eyes, and whatever you say to me I will give. 12) Ask me ever so much dowry and gift, and I will give according to what you say to me; but give me the young woman as a wife."

13) But the sons of Jacob answered Shechem and Hamor his father, and spoke deceitfully, because he had defiled Dinah their sister. 14) And they said to them, "We cannot do this thing, to give our sister to one who is uncircum-cised, for that would be a reproach to us. 15) But on this condition we will consent to you: if you will become as we are, if every male of you is circumcised. 16) then we will give our daughters to you, and we will take your daughters to us; and we will dwell with you, and we will become one people. 17) But if you will not heed us and be circumcised, then we will take our daughter and be gone."

Any questions?

Clarifications:

Jacob's family: Genesis 29:31-30:24; 35:16-18

Son	Daughter	Mother:
Reuben		_____
Simeon		_____
Levi		_____
Judah		_____
Naphtali		_____
Gad		_____
Asher		_____
Issachar		_____
Zebulun		_____
	Dinah	
Joseph		_____
Benjamin		_____

Let's think about it.

1. Where does Dinah fit in Jacob's family?

2. What influence could her position in the family have had on her foolish decision?

3. Describe Dinah. (Genesis 34:2-3)

4. Describe Shechem. (Gen 34:2, 3, 8,)

5. Where is Dinah while her brothers are negotiating with Hamor and Shechem?

The rest of the story:

Hamor had to do a lot of tall talking to please his son. All the men of the city had to do was to undergo circumcision and Jacob's prosperity would become part of their economy. Amazingly, they agreed. Foolishly, they trusted Jacob's sons and all went through the ceremony on the same day.

Did the Scriptures mention that Jacob's sons spoke "deceitfully?" They had planned ahead. If the city of Shechem took them up on their offer, every man of the city would be incapacitated in three days. And that is the day Dinah's two older brothers, Simeon and Levi, attacked the city with swords.

Two men against a city, seeking vengeance and rescue for their baby sister. They murdered very man, including Shechem and Hamor. They found the harem room and freed Dinah from her keepers. Then they looted the city, confiscated all the livestock, and took the women and children captive.

Did they expect a triumphant home-coming? Instead they faced Jacob's rebuke. He feared retribution from the surrounding tribes. Hear him weeping. See him wringing his hands. He and his household would surely be destroyed.

But Simeon and Levi justified their actions: "Should he treat our sister like a harlot?"

Apparently Jacob never forgave Simeon and Levi for
endangering the family. In his final blessing on his sons, he
put these two brothers together and actually cursed them
instead of blessing them.

What about Dinah?

The scriptures do not tell us anything more. The shame of
being raped – defiled – probably prevented her from
marriage in her culture. It certainly would have prevented a
"prosperous" marriage. She may well have become the
"mother" to Rachel's children: Joseph, a toddler at the
time, and Benjamin, who would be born in a few short
months. If that is what happened, she had a rich part in the
education of Joseph, one of the most godly men in the
Bible.

What's in it for me?

1. Relate Ephesians 2:8-9 to painful memories.

2. Relate 1 John 1:9 to personal struggles.

3. What have you done with the painful memories from your past?

4.What can you glean from Dinah's story to help you counsel younger women?

5.What do you personally take away from Dinah's story for your own life?

6.Write an appropriate title for this lesson.

Application:

Most of us carry shameful events in our past that we would like to forget about, some brought on by our own foolishness and others because of someone else's sin. The Apostle Paul counsels us: "…forgetting those things which are behind and reaching forward to those things which are ahead, I press toward the goal for the prize of the upward call of God in Christ Jesus."

Wherever you fit in this story, God is your rescuer. His grace is sufficient to cover any and all defilement. (Ephesians 2:8-9.) His mercies are new every morning. (Lamentations 3:23.) If we confess our sins He is faithful and just to forgive us our sins and to cleanse us from all unrighteousness. (1 John 1:9.) We need to apply these verses to our own lives and then live and share them with the women God brings into our sphere of influence.

Response:

Has God touched your heart or taught you something new in this study of Dinah? Write your prayer of response to Him.

For Further Study:
Genesis 34; 46:15;
Joseph's story: Genesis 37, 39-48, 50.

Miriam: _____

Just Imagine

You are a pre-teen slave girl in ancient Egypt. You've heard the stories about your family's prominence in the past. The original prime minister was actually a great, great, ever-so-great uncle of yours. But that was nearly 400 years ago. The Hebrews are no longer friends of Pharaoh.

As a matter of fact, the new Pharaoh is so worried about his slaves, he has ordered all the boy babies to be killed. That is beyond sad. It is terrifying. Your baby brother Aaron was born before that edict, but now a new baby has come into your family. The midwives, of course, have not obeyed Pharaoh's terrible orders to kill him.

So your job is to help hide the baby. At first that wasn't a hard job. Just watch the baby. The moment he looks like he's about to fuss, grab him up and take him to Mother to nurse.

But he's three months old now. Mother worries that we will no longer be able to stifle those cries before an Egyptian guard hears him. Pharaoh is angry that his orders are ignored. He has commanded his guards to find those infants and toss them into the Nile River.

However, Mother has a plan. She says God gave her the plan and that God is going to use this child to do something special for His people. She carefully chooses a basket just big enough to make a bed for the baby. She has Father bring asphalt and pitch when he returns from building Pharaoh's newest city. You watch as she painstakingly covers the outside of the basket with the gooey tar. Then she lets it dry overnight.

In the early morning, Mother sends you to find soft rags to line the inside of the basket. She gathers little Aaron and you to pray as she places the baby in the basket.

"Now it's up to Jehovah," she says. "Pharaoh says to throw the babies into the Nile. That's what we'll do." And she walks with you down to the river, places the basket-boat on the water, and directs you to watch and pray that Pharaoh's daughter will find and rescue your baby brother.

What are your thoughts?

What are your fears? Why?

What do you plan to do when the princess comes to bathe?

Read All About Miriam:

Exodus 2:1)And a man of the house of Levi went and took as wife a daughter of Levi. 2) So the woman conceived and bore a son. And when she saw that he was a beautiful child, she hid him three months. 3) But when she could no longer hide him, she took an ark of the bulrushes for him, daubed it with asphalt and pitch, put the child in it, and laid it in the reeds by the river's bank. 4) And his sister stood afar off, to know what would be done to him.

5) Then the daughter of Pharaoh came down to bathe at the river. And her maidens walked along the riverside; and when she saw the ark among the reeds, she sent her maid to get it. 6) And when she opened it, she saw the child, and behold, the baby wept. So she had compassion on him, and said, "This is one of the Hebrews' children."

7) Then his sister said to Pharaoh's daughter, "Shall I go and call a nurse for you from the Hebrew women, that she may nurse the child for you?"

8) And Pharaoh's daughter said to her, "Go."

So the maiden went and called the child's mother.

9) Then Pharaoh's daughter said to her, "Take this child away and nurse him for me, and I will give you your wages."

So the woman took the child and nursed him. 10) And the child grew, and she brought him to Pharaoh's daughter, and he became her son. So she called his name Moses, saying, "Because I drew him out of the water."

Any questions?

Clarifications:

Miriam is an alternative form of Mary. They both mean bitter. She may have been so named because of the bitter life into which she was born.

Moses means "to draw out."

We are not sure how old Miriam was at Moses' birth. Some commentators say as young as seven, some as old as twelve.

Let's think about it.

1. Describe Jochebed. (Miriam's mother)

2. Describe Miriam.

3. Describe the princess.

4. Can you think of any other ways Jochebed (Miriam's mother) could have protected her child?

5. How important was it for Miriam to follow directions and even think on her feet?

6. We know the first years of a child's life are his most important learning years. Jochebed had Moses' full attention at least until he was weaned, either in her home or at the palace. How long do you think that was? What do you think she taught him?

7. By saving Moses' life, they lost him from their family. Or did they? What kind of communication do you think they would have been able to maintain?

The rest of the story:

Life in the ghetto continued. The older Moses grew, the less they saw of him. Miriam may have married. The Bible doesn't tell us, so we don't really know. Tradition says she was married to Hur, the man who helped Aaron support Moses during a battle on the way to the promised land.

Brother Moses received the best education available in the world. Yet he still knew his roots. The slaves knew about his dramatic rescue and often talked about how God was probably going to use this man to rescue them from slavery. Joseph – 400 years before – had told them to take his bones with them when they left Egypt. Surely it was time.

Imagine Miriam's fears when she heard that her brother Moses had killed a slave driver. Then, the next day, when Moses was on his way again to visit the family, he tried to arbitrate between two fighting Hebrews and he realized his violent act was known. Just a quick stop at Jochebed and Aram's house and then he disappeared into the desert. It would be forty more years before she heard from her brother again.

But one day Aaron felt he should go find him. And God
had directed Moses to return. So they met on the way and
returned to Egypt together. Then followed days of
increased servitude. God sent plagues in Egypt (but not in
Goshen, where the slaves lived). Finally God struck dead
all the firstborn of Egypt and told his people to march out.
The Egyptians they worked for were so glad to get rid of
them, they filled their hands with jewels and other things
they might need for the journey.

Up days and down days. Just when they thought they were
safe, news came that Pharaoh had changed his mind again.
This time they were in more trouble than ever: their backs
against the Red Sea, unarmed, facing Pharaoh's charioted
army. Panic!

Moses didn't know what to do – but he did know Who to
ask. God gave him directions that would open the sea.
Moses obeyed and two million slaves followed him on a
dry path through the Red Sea.

But the chariots were still coming! Panic again! Under
God's direction, Moses turned to the sea, stretched out his
hand, and the waters returned, crashing down on the entire
Egyptian army. Free men watched in wonder as their spent
fears washed up on the shores.

Miriam was there. Moses led in a song of praise to God.
The people were stunned. Then 90-year-old Miriam took
up her timbrel and began a victory dance. One by one the
women of Israel picked up their timbrels and expressed
their relief with singing and dancing.

Miriam was called a prophetess (Exodus 15:20). Apparently God used her to counsel and help in the administration of the multitude of Israelites. Unfortunately, her position caused an attitude of pride, for after a couple of years she began grumbling to Aaron about Moses' leadership.

It started as a family concern. Moses had married an Ethiopian woman. Miriam didn't think that was right. But she went further to undermine his position, asking, "Has the Lord indeed spoken only through Moses? Has He not spoken through us also?"

I love the fact that Moses didn't respond. But God did – with anger. He called the three of them to a conference where he vindicated Moses and struck Miriam with leprosy. Imagine the scene: Miriam, white with leprosy; Aaron pleading with Moses to forgive them and pray for Miriam's healing.

Graciously, Moses forgave and prayed. But God replied that she must at least endure a week's quarantine outside the camp. We hear of no more foolishness from Miriam or Aaron.

What's in it for me?

1. God gave a lot of space (four books) to Moses' story, and Miriam is a part of that. There are many lessons to be learned: trust, training children, humility. Can you name some others?

2. One major lesson from Miriam's life is being willing to use God-given abilities for Him. How are you doing that in your life?

3.Do you need to make or renew a commitment in this area?

4. The second major lesson is humility. How are you doing in this area?

5.How can you teach younger women this quality?

6.What do you personally take away from Miriam's life for your own?

7.Write an appropriate title for this lesson.

Application:

Wherever we are on life's journey, we're always learning to trust God more. Whatever responsibilities He has given us, we need to constantly remind ourselves of our position before him. We are redeemed slaves. All the tools we have to work with came from Him. To God be the glory.

Response:

Has something from this study of Miriam touched your life? Take a minute and write your prayer of response to God.

For Further Study:
Exodus 2:1-10; 15:20-21; Numbers 12:1-15; 20:1; 26:59; Deuteronomy 24:9; Micah 6:4

Rahab: _____

Just Imagine

What do you already know about Rahab? Describe what you think may have brought her to this occupation/lifestyle.

How might her profession have influenced her family relationships? Friendships?

What advantages would Rahab have as the city's innkeeper?

What were her fears living in a fortified city among warring tribes and hearing reports of Israel's advances?

Read All About Rahab:

Joshua 2:1) Now Joshua the son of Nun sent out two men from Acacia Grove to spy secretly, saying, "Go, view the land, especially Jericho."

So they went, and came to the house of a harlot named Rahab, and lodged there. 2) And it was told the king of Jericho, saying, "Behold, men have come here tonight from the children of Israel to search out the country."

3) So the king of Jericho sent to Rahab, saying, "Bring out the men who have come to you, who have entered your house, for they have come to search out all the country."

4) Then the woman took the two men and hid them. So she said, "Yes, the men came to me, but I did not know where they were from. 5) "And it happened as the gate was being shut, when it was dark, that the men went out. Where the men went I do not know; pursue them quickly, for you may overtake them."

6) (But she had brought them up to the roof and hidden them with the stalks of flax, which she had laid in order on the roof.)

7) Then the men pursued them by the road to the Jordan, to the fords. And as soon as those who pursued them had gone out, they shut the gate.

8) Now before they lay down, she came up to them on the roof, 9) and said to the men: "I know that the Lord has given you the land, that the terror of you has fallen on us, and that all the inhabitants of the land are fainthearted because of you. 10) "For we have heard how the Lord dried up the water of the Red Sea for you when you came out of Egypt, and what you did to the two kings of the Amorites who were on the other side of the Jordan, Sihon and Og, whom you utterly destroyed. 11) "And as soon as we heard these things, our hearts melted; neither did there remain any more courage in anyone because of you, for the Lord your God, He is God in heaven above and on earth beneath. 12) "Now therefore, I beg you, swear to me by the Lord, since I have shown you kindness, that you also will show kindness to my father's house, and give me a true token. 13) "and spare my father, my mother, my brothers, my sisters, and all that they have, and deliver our lives from death."

14) So the men answered her, "Our lives for yours, if none of you tell this business of ours. And it shall be, when the Lord has given us the land, that we will deal kindly and truly with you."

15) Then she let them down by a rope through the window, for her house was on the city wall; she dwelt on the wall. 16) And she said to them, "Get to the mountain, lest the pursuers meet you. Hide there three days, until the pursuers have returned. Afterward you may go your way."

17) So the men said to her, "We will be blameless of this oath of yours which you have made us swear, 18) "unless, when we come into the land, you bind this line of scarlet cord in the window through which you let us down, and unless you bring your father, your mother, your brothers, and all your father's household to your own home. 19) "So it shall be that whoever goes outside the doors of your house into the street, his blood shall be on his own head, and we will be guiltless. And whoever is with you in the house, his blood shall be on our head if a hand is laid on him. 20) "And if you tell this business of ours, then we will be free from your oath, which you made us swear."

21) Then she said, "According to your words, so be it."

And she sent them away, and they departed. And she bound the scarlet cord in the window. 22) They departed and went to the mountain, and stayed there three days until the pursuers returned. The pursuers sought them all along the way, but did not find them.

23) So the two men returned, descended from the mountain, and crossed over; and they came to Joshua the son of Nun, and told him all that had befallen them. 24) And they said to Joshua, "Truly the Lord has delivered all the land into our hands, for indeed all the inhabitants of the country are fainthearted because of us."

Any questions?

Clarifications:

Rahab – from "Ra," an Egyptian god; means "insolence," "fierceness," or "broad," "spaciousness."

Rahab the **harlot** – lodging in an inn often included prostitutes at no extra charge

The **inn on the wall** – fortified city walls were often actually double walls, twenty to thirty feet apart. Homes (with their businesses) were built into the walls. The flat tops were used for work areas and relief from summer's heat.

Flax – maybe an indication that Rahab sold linen

Let's think about it.

1. What did Rahab know about Israel?

2. What had she decided about her own survival because of this knowledge?

3. There's always the question of Rahab lying to the king's messengers. Compare with James 2:24-26. What about those lies?

4. We think of grace as a New Testament concept. (1 Corinthians 6:9-11) What did the Israelites know about grace? (Exodus 34:1-9)

The rest of the story:

Rahab waited. Her first priority was to persuade the rest of her family to move into her inn. Every morning she reminded them to stay close and be sure they were beneath her roof, especially if anything unusual happened. Every morning she checked to make sure the red cord was visible from her window.

She eavesdropped on every table conversation. Three days after the spy incident there was no report of their capture. Then, four days after that the news came that Israel had crossed the Jordan. At flood stage? Now she knew for sure that Israel's God was real. He was doing the same sort of miracles He did at the beginning of Israel's escape from Egypt.

There followed days of quiet – no reports. From her rooftop, Rahab could sometimes catch a glimpse of the edge of Israel's camp. What was going on out there?

Then one morning Jericho was aroused by the sound of trumpets and marching feet. A huge multitude marched behind the trumpeters. Once around Jericho and then they disappeared back to their camp. Immediately her inn filled with worried citizens. Speculations and threats continued into the night.

Next day? A repeat. What were these strange people up to? And they did it the third day. And the fourth.

By the end of the week the Jerichoites expected this daily "show of force." If that was Israel's way of conquering their city, Jericho's citizens could almost laugh it off.

But the seventh day brought a change. The multitude continued their march: not just once around, but two times, then three. On and on they marched. The whole town gathered on the rooftops, wondering about this strange activity.

Rahab sensed the end. She didn't know how it would happen but she urged her family members to stay inside her home. Israel marched on and on: seven times around the great walled city.

Then the invaders stopped and stood stock still for a moment, completely surrounding the city. Their commander pumped his fist and the entire multitude shouted and ran toward Jericho. Jericho's walls began to shake and crumble. Citizens ran screaming to the city center, blinded by the dust and dodging debris. In a few minutes, over flattened walls, the Israelites were upon them.

Remember the spies? Joshua directed them to honor their promise and rescue Rahab, her parents, her siblings, her nieces and nephews. They took them back to their camp, away from the fighting where they were safe.

The story doesn't end there. Rahab was anxious to learn more about this true and living God. Salmon, one of the spies, may have been the one who was happy to teach her. Rahab found grace among God's people. Her gratitude led her to worship Israel's God. Somehow, mutual respect between her and Salmon blossomed into love. We next read of them at the end of the book of Ruth: husband and wife, parents of the successful and godly Boaz, the rescuer and husband of Ruth.

What's in it for me?

1. What quality enabled Rahab to survive Jericho's fall? (Hebrews 11:31)

2. How did Rahab exhibit her faith? (James 2:24-26)

3. What does faith have to do with getting rid of a sinful lifestyle? (Ephesians 2:8-9)

4. What kind of parents were Salmon and Rahab? (Ruth 2:4)

5. What do you personally take from Rahab for your own life?

6.Write an appropriate title for this lesson.

Application:

When we come to Christ our lives change. We hate our former sin and any tendencies to return to that life. It may take a while, but acquaintances usually change their view of us. However, Rahab, changed as she must have been, is always referred to as Rahab the Harlot. Maybe, every time she heard that, she inwardly praised God that it was no longer so. When we are confronted with our past, we also need to confess and lay it again at God's feet and praise Him that it's no longer so.

Response:
Has something from this study of Rahab touched your life? Take a minute and write your prayer of response to God.

For Further Study:
Joshua 2:2-21; 6:17-25; Ruth 4:13-22; Matthew 1:5; Hebrews 11:31; James 2:24-26

Ruth: _____

Just Imagine

1. What would cause a beautiful, young, pagan woman to marry into the family of a foreign sojourner?

2. What cultural differences would there be between Moabites and Israelites?

3. What cultural similarities might there be?

4. Why would an Israelite man choose to marry a Moabite woman?

5. What would be the concerns of the Israelite's elderly mother?

6. How might the mother seek to mitigate her concerns?

Read All About Ruth:

Ruth 1:1) Now it came to pass, in the days when the judges ruled, that there was a famine in the land. And a certain man of Bethlehem, Judah, went to dwell in the country of Moab, he and his wife and his two sons. 2) The name of the man was Elimelech, the name of his wife was Naomi, and the names of his two sons were Mahlon and Chilion – Ephrathites of Bethlehem, Judah. And they went to the country of Moab and remained there.

3) Then Elimelech, Naomi's husband, died; and she was left, and her two sons. 4) Now they took wives of the women of Moab: the name of the one was Orpah and the name of the other Ruth. And they dwelt there about ten years.

5) Then both Mahlon and Chilion also died; so the woman survived her two sons and her husband.

6) The she arose with her daughters-in-law that she might return from the country of Moab, for she had heard in the country of Moab that the Lord had visited His people by giving them bread. 7) Therefore she went out from the place where she was, and her two daughters-in-law with her; and they went on the way to return to the land of Judah.

8) And Naomi said to her two daughters-in-law, "Go, return each to her mother's house. The Lord deal kindly with you, as you have dealt with the dead and with me. 9) "The Lord grant that you may find rest, each in the house of her husband."

So she kissed them, and they lifted up their voices and wept, 10) And they said to her, "Surely we will return with you to your people."

11) But Naomi said, "Turn back, my daughters; why will you go with me? Are there still sons in my womb, that they may be your husbands? 12) "Turn back, my daughters, go – for I am too old to have a husband. If I should say I have hope, if I should have a husband tonight and should also bear sons, 13) "would you wait for them till they were grown? Would you restrain yourselves from having husbands: No, my daughters; for it grieves me very much for your sakes that the hand of the Lord has gone out against me!"

14) Then they lifted up their voices and wept again; and Orpah kissed her mother-in-law, but Ruth clung to her.
15) And she said, "Look, your sister-in-law has gone back to her people and to her gods; return after your sister-in-law."

16) But Ruth said: "Entreat me not to leave you,
>> *Or to turn back from following after you;*
>> *For wherever you go, I will go;*
>> *And wherever you lodge, I will lodge;*
>> *Your people shall be my people,*
>> *And your God, my God.*
>> *17) Where you die, I will die,*
>> *And there will I be buried.*
>> *The Lord do so to me, and more also,*
>> *If anything but death parts you and me."*

18) When she saw that she was determined to go with her, she stopped speaking to her.

Any questions?

Clarifications:

Bethlehem – House of Bread and Praise

Elimelech – my God is King

Mahlon – sickly, or mild

Chilion – pining

Orpah – neck???

Ruth – companion, or friend, or satiated

Boaz – quickness or strength

Let's think about it.

1. Who were the Moabites? Genesis 19:30-38; Numbers 22:1-12 (to 25:18); Judges 3:12-30.

2. What would cause an Israelite to seek refuge in enemy territory?

3. Describe Naomi's probable economic status.

4. Verses 16 and 17 are often quoted or sung at weddings. This pledged was originally made from Ruth to
_____.

5. What did Ruth promise Naomi?

6. What was Ruth giving up by going with Naomi?

7. What was she gaining?

The rest of the story:

It's a long walk from Moab to Israel, especially if you're carrying everything you own on your back. Naomi tried to keep the pace up, but she was getting to be an old woman. The closer they came to Bethlehem, the more bitter Naomi's heart became. Only her cheerful daughter-in-law Ruth made life worth living at all. When they finally entered the city they were amazed at the stir their arrival caused. Naomi's old friends barely recognized her. "Is this Naomi?" they asked each other.

Naomi nodded. "Don't call me Naomi," she said. "Call me Mara. For the Almighty has dealt very bitterly with me. I went out full, and the Lord has brought me home again empty. Why do you call me Naomi, since the Lord has testified against me, and the Almighty has afflicted me?"

But she gladly accepted the hugs of her friends and introduced her precious Ruth to them.

At least they had timed it right. Barley harvest was in full swing. As poor people, they had the right to glean in the fields and try to accumulate enough food to get them through the winter. Naomi's pride might keep her from asking her old neighbors for help, but there was no shame in gleaning.

Ruth wouldn't hear of it. "I'll do the gleaning, Mother," she stated. Promptly the next morning Ruth was up before dawn and out to the barley fields. What a day she had. God led her to one of Boaz's fields. He "just happened" to be the richest farmer in Bethlehem. But better than that, he was also a man of integrity, alarmed by the sinful lifestyle of his fellow citizens and concerned for the safety of his workers, and even of the gleaners who followed his harvesters. Ruth's reputation had already preceded her, and Boaz immediately offered his protection and assured her of safety in his fields. He personally saw to her comfort at the noon meal and made sure she had all the grain she could carry home to Naomi at the end of the day.

When Naomi saw the heap of barley, she knew Ruth had come upon a generous farmer. When she heard it was Boaz, her heart leaped with joy and hope. Boaz was a near kinsman of her late husband's. Ruth could appeal to him for her rights as his relative. Naomi made her plan, wisely waiting until the end of barley harvest to put it into effect.

So it was that the evening of threshing, Naomi directed Ruth to Boaz's threshing floor. Ruth followed her directions to the letter. She joined in the feasting, celebrating a great harvest. She watched as fellow gleaners and harvesters one by one disappeared to their homes and Boaz's employees found their guard stations and settled down for the night. Finally Boaz went to his sleeping area. She followed and quietly lay down at his feet.

As Naomi predicted, Boaz awoke in the middle of the night – and there was Ruth lying at his feet. Startled at first, he soon realized her request. She was a near relative and she was asking his redemption.

Quietly, before dawn, he sent her home with a pile of threshed barley and the promise to see what he could do – for there was a kinsman closer to Naomi than he was. That very day he contacted the other relative, convened a committee of elders at the city gate and offered Ruth to the relative.

At first the man was interested. Naomi still owned Elimelech's property. But then Boaz reported that the property came with an even greater prize: Ruth, the Moabitess. The nearer relative was already a married man and was in no way interested in disrupting his household. Employing the custom of the time, he removed his sandal (signifying sealing the deal) and told Boaz to buy the property (and Ruth) for himself.

Activity at the city gate always generated interest from the citizens. A great crowd had gathered and Boaz's reputation passed on to Ruth, whom he had chosen to marry. Rejoicing and good wishes continued. The wedding happened quickly, and within a year little Obed was born to the happy couple.

Of course, Boaz included Naomi in his family, as welcome as his own mother, Rahab, whose death he still mourned. When little Obed was born, Naomi naturally became his nursemaid, showing him off to all her old friends who clucked and baby-talked and passed him around, endlessly.

So it is that God, in His grace, not only brought the harlot Rahab into the ancestral line of Christ, but also one from the cursed nation of Moab. Ruth is a love story that goes far beyond the two lovers involved.

What's in it for me?

1.Describe Ruth. (1:16-18; 2:2-23; 3:1-18; 4:13-17)

2. Describe Naomi. (1:1-22; 2:18-23; 3:1-5, 16-18; 4:14-17)

3. Describe Boaz. (2:1-16; 3:7-18; 4:1-13)

4. What kind of love story is this? Describe the relationships you see in the book of Ruth.

5. What do you personally take away from Ruth for your own life?

6. Write an appropriate title for this lesson on Ruth.

Application:

The Book of Ruth is a positive picture in the midst of an extremely perilous time of Israel's history. In Ruth we see hope. Hope of grace even after running from hard times.

Hope of love in the midst of grief. Hope that godliness can prevail even in a godless society. Hope of redemption, even for someone outside the family of God. Hope that bitterness will be replaced with fulfillment.

Response:

Has something from this study of Ruth touched your life? Take a minute and write your prayer of response to God.

For Further Study:
Matthew 1:1-16; Luke 3:23-38.

*Abigail:*_____

Just Imagine

You've got it all! You are not only beautiful, you are married to the richest sheep rancher in northern Israel. When you married him (even though you had no say in the decision), what were your expectations?

Actually, you have more than you bargained for. Your rich husband is an abusive alcoholic. As a Jewish woman, how do you cope?

Read All About Abigail:

1 Samuel 25:14) Now one of the young men told Abigail, Nabal's wife, saying, "Look, David sent messengers from the wilderness to greet our master, and he reviled them. 15) "But the men were very good to us, and we were not hurt, nor did we miss anything as long as we accompanied them, when we were in the fields. 16) "They were a wall to us both by night and day, all the time we were with them keeping the sheep. 17) "Now therefore, know and consider what you will do, for harm is determined against our master and against all his household. For he is such a scoundrel that one cannot speak to him."

18) Then Abigail made haste and took two hundred loaves of bread, two skins of wine, five sheep already dressed, five seahs of roasted grain, one hundred clusters of raisins, and two hundred cakes of figs, and loaded them on donkeys. 19) And she said to her servants, "Go on before me; see, I am coming after you."

But she did not tell her husband Nabal.

20) So it was, as she rode on the donkey, that she went down under cover of the hill; and there were David and his men, coming down toward her, and she met them.

21) Now David had said, "Surely in vain I have protected all that this fellow has in the wilderness, so that nothing was missed of all that belongs to him. And he has repaid me evil for good. 22) "May God do so, and more also, to the enemies of David, if I leave one male of all who belong to him by morning light."

23) Now when Abigail saw David, she dismounted quickly from the donkey, fell on her face before David, and bowed down to the ground. 24) So she fell at his feet and said, "On me, my lord, on me let this iniquity be! And please let your maidservant speak in your ears, and hear the words of your maidservant.

25) "Please, let not my lord regard this scoundrel Nabal. For as his name is, so is he: Nabal is his name and folly is with him! But I, your maidservant, did not see the young men of my lord whom you sent.

26) "Now therefore, my lord, as the Lord lives and as your soul lives, since the Lord has held you back from coming to bloodshed and from avenging yourself with your own hand, now then, let your enemies and those who seek harm for my lord be as Nabal. 27) "And now this present which your maidservant has brought to my lord, let it be given to the young men who follow my lord. 28) "Please forgive the trespass of your maidservant. For the Lord will certainly make for my lord an enduring house, because my lord fights the battles of the Lord, and evil is not found in you throughout your days.

29) "Yet a man has risen to pursue you and seek your life, but the life of my lord shall be bound in the bundle of the living with the Lord your God; and the lives of your enemies He shall sling out, as from the pocket of a sling. 30) "And it shall come to pass, when the Lord has done for my lord according to all the good that He has spoken concerning you, and has appointed you ruler over Israel, 31) "That this will be no grief to you, nor offense of heart to my lord, either that you have shed blood without cause, or that my lord has avenged himself. But when the Lord has dealt well with my lord, then remember your maidservant."

32) Then David said to Abigail, "Blessed by the Lord God of Israel, who sent you this day to meet me! 33) "And blessed is your advice and blessed are you, because you have kept me this day from coming to bloodshed and from avenging myself with my own hand. 34) "For indeed, as the Lord God of Israel lives, who has kept me back from hurting you, unless you had hurried and come to meet me, surely by morning light no males would have been left to Nabal."

35) So David received from her hand what she had brought him, and said to her, "Go up in peace to your house. See, I have heeded your voice and respected your person."

Any questions?

Clarifications:

Abigail – father or cause of joy

Nabal – a fool

Maon – Area near Mount Carmel in northern Israel

Let's think about it.

1. Describe Abigail. (1 Samuel 25:3, 19)

2. Describe Nabal. (1 Samuel 25: 2-3, 25)

3. What was David's request of Nabal?

4. What was Nabal's response?

5. What did David intend to do about Nabal's response?

6. How did Abigail address the problem?

7.What was the result of her actions?

8. What did Abigail prophesy? (1 Samuel 25:28-31)

The rest of the story:

Abigail saved the day. However, she still had to face her belligerent husband. Nabal may have been a fool, but Abigail certainly was not. She intended to tell him what she had done as soon as she returned from delivering supplies to David. However, Nabal was too drunk to talk to. She waited until morning when Nabal had a hangover, but his brain was no longer muddled with alcohol.

Predictably, Nabal responded with oaths and threats, all the while slowly realizing his wise partner had probably spared him and his entire operation from death. While Abigail cowered near the doorway, Nabal suddenly clutched his chest, groaned loudly, and fell headlong to the floor.

Good wife that she was, Abigail called for servants and had him carried to his bedchamber. For days she cared for him, but the tenth day he stopped breathing. Nabal was dead.

Now what should she do? It is probable that Nabal's family (they had no children) could come and possess her home. She might convince them to let her stay there and help run the household.

Or she could return to the home of her birth. She would be welcome there, but there would be nothing for her to do.

If Nabal had a brother, he had the right to marry her, and she had the right to demand it. However, she wanted nothing to do with any man in Nabal's family. God had answered her prayers to end this marriage in a way she had never considered.

David's men still hid in the valley near Nabal's ranch. Soon they reported Nabal's death to David. He blessed God for taking care of his Nabal problem, and then sent messengers to propose marriage to Abigail.

Abigail gave up her beautiful home to join David and his six hundred soldiers and their families in the wilderness. She would be David's third wife, but only Ahinoam was actually with David's company. Abigail brought five of her maidens with her, as becoming a wife of a king – whom she had prophesied David would one day become.

Several years elapsed before David actually became king in Hebron. Before that, at the end of their "hiding out" time, David found refuge for his followers in Ziklag, a Philistine town. While David and most of the soldiers were away fighting, Amalekites raided Ziklag, capturing all who were left in the city and looting it, including David's two wives. David soon returned and pursued them with 400 of his men. He recovered all their people and belongings.

With what joy and relief Abigail and Ahinoam settled into the royal home in Hebron. Warfare with the house of Saul continued for seven years. During that time Ahinoam bore David his first son, Amnon, Abigail bore Chileab, and David married Maacah, Haggith, Abital, and Eglah, who each bore a son. David also sent for Michal, daughter of Saul (his first wife), to be returned to him.

Once David was crowned king of all Israel, they moved to Jerusalem. Many years later Bathsheba also became a wife of David.

It is hard to imagine living in a polygamous family. Besides the wives, there were concubines. Abigail's confidence in God's control of David's life, as well as her God-given wisdom and quick thinking, doubtless gave her comfort and leadership in David's household. We read no more of her or of her child. We can only guess how much influence she had in David's life and the lives of his children.

What's in it for me?

We sometimes feel we are in desperate situations with no way out. Married to a brutal man, Abigail surely prayed for strength and a way of escape, and God answered. She understood God's plan for her nation through David. That gave her courage to confront both David and Nabal. Walking close to God gives us courage to act, for we have the insight to hear His voice and the confidence to do what He tells us. What a lesson!

Application:

1. When have you felt so desperate that you could only call on God for help? What happened?

2. How can you use what God has taught you to encourage other women – or children or grandchildren – to draw closer to God?

3. What do you personally take away from Abigail for your own life?

4. Write a title for this chapter on Abigail.

Response:
Has something from this study of Abigail touched your life? Take a minute and write your prayer of response to God.

For Further Study:
1 Samuel 25; 1 Samuel 27:3; 30:5, 18; 2 Samuel 2:2; 3:3; 1 Chronicles 3:1

Bathsheba: _____

Just Imagine

It's the age-old question: Was Bathsheba a victim – or a seductress? Why do you think so?

Read All About Bathsheba:

2 Samuel 11:1) It happened in the spring of the year, at the time when kings go out to battle, that David sent Joab and his servants with him, and all Israel; and they destroyed the people of Ammon and besieged Rabbah. But David remained at Jerusalem.

Then it happened one evening that David arose from his bed and walked on the roof of the king's house. And from the roof he saw a woman bathing, and the woman was very beautiful to behold. 3) So David sent and inquired about the woman. And someone said, "Is this not Bathsheba, the daughter of Eliam, the wife of Uriah the Hittite?"

4) Then David sent messengers, and took her; and she came to him, and he lay with her, for she was cleansed from her impurity; and she returned to her house. 5) And the woman conceived; so she sent and told David, and said, "I am with child."

6) Then David sent to Joab, saying, "Send me Uriah the Hittite." And Joab sent Uriah to David.

7) When Uriah had come to him, David asked how Joab was doing, and how the people were doing, and how the war prospered. 8) And David said to Uriah, "Go down to your house and wash your feet."

So Uriah departed from the king's house, and a gift of food from the king followed him. 9) But Uriah slept at the door of the king's house with all the servants of his lord, and did not go down to his house.

10) So when they told David, saying, "Uriah did not go down to his house," David said to Uriah, "Did you not come from a journey? Why did you not go down to your house?"

11) And Uriah said to David, "The ark and Israel and Judah are dwelling in tents, and my lord Joab and the servants of my lord are encamped in the open fields. Shall I then go to my house to eat and drink, and to lie with my wife? As you live, and as your soul lives, I will not do this thing."

12) Then David said to Uriah, "Wait here today also, and tomorrow I will let you depart."

*So Uriah remained in Jerusalem that day and the next. 13)
Now when David called him, he ate and drank before him;
and he made him drunk. And at evening he went out to lie
on his bed with the servants of his lord, but he did not go
down to his house.*

*14) In the morning it happened that David wrote a letter to
Joab and sent it by the hand of Uriah. 15) And he wrote in
the letter, saying, "Set Uriah in the forefront of the hottest
battle, and retreat from him, that he may be struck down
and die."*

*16) So it was, while Joab besieged the city, that he assigned
Uriah to a place where he knew there were valiant men.
17) Then the men of the city came out and fought with
Joab. And some of the people of the servants of David fell;
and Uriah the Hittite died also.*

*18) Then Joab sent and told David all the things
concerning the war, 19) and charged the messenger,
saying, "When you have finished telling the matters of the
war to the king, ...21b) – then you shall say, 'Your servant
Uriah the Hittite is dead also.'"*

*22) So the messenger went, and came and told David all
that Joab had sent by him. 23) And the messenger said to
David, "Surely the men prevailed against us and came out
to us in the field; then we drove them back as far as the
entrance of the gate. 24) The archers shot from the wall at
your servants; and some of the king's servants are dead,
and your servant Uriah the Hittite is dead also."*

25) Then David said to the messenger, "Thus you shall say to Joab: 'Do not let this thing displease you, for the sword devours one as well as another. Strengthen your attack against the city, and overthrow it.' So encourage him."

26) When the wife of Uriah heard that Uriah her husband was dead, she mourned for her husband. 27) And when her mourning was over, David sent and brought her to his house, and she became his wife and bore him a son. But the thing that David had done displeased the Lord.

Any questions?

Clarifications:

Bathsheba – means daughter of an oath or daughter of abundance

Bathsheba's family: granddaughter of Ahithophel, one of David's advisors who sided with Absalom in the later insurrection, likely because of David's affair with Bathsheba.

Bathing – probably ritual cleansing marking the end of her monthly period

Walked on the roof – sleeping chambers were often on the flat rooftop, especially in warm weather.

Hittites – citizens of or mercenaries from the Anatolian or neo-Hittite Empire of Syria, or possibly an unrelated group living in Canaan

Uriah – means the Lord is light

Let's think about it.

1. Why was David not with his troops fighting Rabbah? (2 Samuel 12:31; 21:15-17)

2. Where was Bathsheba when David saw her from his rooftop?

3. Could Bathsheba have refused to go to David? (Esther 1:10-12, 19-22)

4. What is David's response to Bathsheba's announcement?

5. What alternatives might David have had?

6. Why doesn't David's plan work?

7. Seductress or victim? (2 Samuel 12:1-14)

The rest of the story:

I would not have wanted to be Nathan. God sent him to confront David with his sin. David may have thought that his sin was hidden. Maybe his subjects would just think he was a good king for taking in the pregnant wife of the fallen soldier Uriah.

But God sent Nathan to David with a parable about a rich man who took a poor man's only pet lamb and served it for dinner to his guests. Tenderhearted David was incensed. He condemned the rich man to death and ordered him to repay the poor man four times.

"You are the man!" Nathan declared. Then he reminded David of all God had given him – including several wives – and of adultery and murder. And he announced that David's household would deal with murders and adversity from then on – including the death of his and Bathsheba's son.

David, as king, could have executed Nathan on the spot. Instead he finally confessed his sins and pled with God for the healing of his son.

Where was Bathsheba in all this turmoil? According to Nathan's parable, she is the innocent lamb. However, it was her husband who David murdered. David took her as his eighth wife, sheltering her from gossip and even possible stoning. It was her infant son that died in her arms.

Had God forgotten her? Surely she wondered what would become of her. Apparently she became David's favorite wife. God sent them another son, the wise Solomon who extended Israel's reign the farthest it has ever been. Solomon means "peaceable." However, Nathan (God's prophet) called him Jedidiah, which means "beloved of the Lord."

When Absalom attempted to take over the throne, the Bible does not tell exactly what David's wives did. The concubines were left in Jerusalem, but the wives probably had to escape with David. Bathsheba, as the youngest wife, may have had great responsibilities in caring for the rest of them. At that time she had four sons and possibly daughters.

As David aged, Bathsheba still had great rapport with him. When Adonijah led his insurrection, we find her boldly reminding David of his earlier promise to make Solomon king. David immediately rallied and crowned Solomon, effectively ending Adonijah's revolt.

Her final act in Scripture was to make a request of Solomon, who received her like a queen and said he would not refuse anything she asked. However, he did refuse her, because she asked a favor for Adonijah which Solomon had to deny in order to keep his kingdom.

What a life! What can we learn from her?

What's in it for me?

Like Bathsheba, sometimes we fear to make the best decisions. Surely Bathsheba's life would have taken a different turn if she had refused David's advances. However, once again we can see how God works things for good even in the midst of what appears very evil to us (Romans 8:28). We can gain a heart of wisdom (Psalm 90:12) as we add to our days.

Application:

1. What have you learned from the choices you have made?

2. How can we gain wisdom?

3. How can you – like Bathsheba – pass this wisdom on to others?

4.What do you personally take away from Bathsheba for your own life?

4. Write a title for this lesson on Bathsheba.

Response:

Has something from this study of Bathsheba touched your life? Take a minute and write your prayer of response to God.

For Further Study:
2 Samuel 11, 12; 12:24; 15:12; 1 Kings 1, 2; 1 Chronicles 3:5; Matthew 1:6

*Jezebel:*_____

Just Imagine

The glorious reign of Solomon ended sixty years ago.
Solomon's not-so-wise son's selfish acts caused the
northern kingdom (Israel) to separate from the southern
kingdom (Judah). You live in the north, far from the temple
where God's people were directed to worship. Each king of
Israel has been worse than the last, inviting more and more
idolatry into the land. Occasional prophets have come
through, reminding you and your people of your history
with Jehovah.

You thought Omri was a bad, idolatrous king. Now his son
Ahab has taken over. Omri was bad, but Ahab is horrible.
He has decided to cement relations with the Phoenicians by
marrying their princess, the priestess of Baal, Jezebel.
Jezebel is pushing her god of fertility and fire on your
country, hunting down and killing the prophets of Jehovah,
and building temples to Baal. She has put 450 of these
prophets on government salary.

What are your thoughts about the future of your country?
About your own ability to worship? About your rights as a
citizen?

Read All About Jezebel:

1 Kings 16:29) In the thirty-eighth year of Asa king of Judah, Ahab the son of Omri became king over Israel; and Ahab the son of Omri reigned over Israel in Samaria twenty-two years. 30) Now Ahab the son of Omri did evil in the sight of the Lord, more than all who were before him. 31) And it came to pass, as though it had been a trivial thing for him to walk in the sins of Jeroboam the son of Nebat, that he took as wife Jezebel the daughter of Ethbaal, king of the Sidonians; and he went and served Baal and worshiped him. 32) Then he set up an altar for Baal in the temple of Baals, which he had built in Samaria. 33) And Ahab made a wooden image. Ahab did more to provoke the Lord God of Israel to anger than all the kings of Israel who were before him.

1 Kings 17:1) And Elijah the Tishbite, of the inhabitants of Gilead, said to Ahab, "As the Lord God of Israel lives, before whom I stand, there shall not be dew nor rain these years, except at my word."

2) Then the word of the Lord came to him, saying, 3) "Get away from here and turn eastward, and hide by the Brook Cherith, which flows into the Jordan…"

1 Kings 18:1) And it came to pass after many days that the word of the Lord came to Elijah, in the third year, saying, "Go, present yourself to Ahab, and I will send rain on the earth."

2) So Elijah went to present himself to Ahab; and there was a severe famine in Samaria. 3) And Ahab had called Obadiah, who was in charge of his house. (Now Obadiah feared the Lord greatly. 4) For so it was, while Jezebel massacred the prophets of the Lord, that Obadiah had taken one hundred prophets and hidden them, fifty to a cave, and had fed them with bread and water.)

17) Then it happened, when Ahab saw Elijah, that Ahab said to him, "Is that you, O troubler of Israel?"

18) And he answered, "I have not troubled Israel, but you and your father's house have, in that you have forsaken the commandments of the Lord and have followed the Baals. 19) Now therefore, send and gather all Israel to me on Mount Carmel, and four hundred and fifty prophets of Baal, and the four hundred prophets of Asherah, who eat at Jezebel's table."

20) So Ahab sent for all the children of Israel, and gathered the prophets together on Mount Carmel.

36) And it came to pass, at the time of the offering of the evening sacrifice, that Elijah the prophet came near and said, "Lord God of Abraham, Isaac, and Israel, let it be known this day that You are God in Israel and I am Your servant, and that I have done all these things at Your word. 37) "Hear me, O Lord, hear me, that this people may know that You are the Lord God, and that You have turned their hearts back to You again."

38) Then the fire of the Lord fell and consumed the burnt sacrifice, and the wood and the stones and the dust, and it licked up the water that was in the trench.

39) Now when all the people saw it they fell on their faces; and they said, "The Lord, He is God! The Lord, He is God!"

40) And Elijah said to them, "Seize the prophets of Baal! Do not let one of them escape!"

So they seized them; and Elijah brought them down to the Brook Kishon and executed them there.

1 Kings 19:1) And Ahab told Jezebel all that Elijah had done, also how he had executed all the prophets with the sword. 2) Then Jezebel sent a messenger to Elijah, saying, "So let the gods do to me, and more also, if I do not make your life as the life of one of them by tomorrow about this time."

3) And when he saw that, he arose and ran for his life, and went to Beersheba, which belongs to Judah, and left his servant there.

Any questions?

Clarifications:

Jezebel – probably means "Where is the Prince (Baal)?" or "The Prince (Baal) exists."

Baal – Phoenician idol, god of fertility and fire. Because Israel did not eradicate the idolatrous Canaanites when they entered the land, they were continually plagued with periods of Baal worship. It included prostitution and even child sacrifice.

Elijah – means "my God is Yahweh."

Tishbite – the area of Gilead from which Elijah came – other side of the Jordan

Ashtoreth or Asherah – goddess of fertility. Like a feminine form of Baal.

Let's think about it.

1. Describe Jezebel. (1 Kings 16:31; 18:4, 13; 19:1-3; 2 Kings 9:30)

2. Describe Ahab. (1 Kings 16:29-33; 17:1; 18:3-6, 16-20, 40-41, 44-45; 19:1)

3. God judged Israel by holding back the rain. How was that a particular affront to the Baal worshipers?

4. Elijah goes into hiding for three years after pronouncing God's judgment. When he comes out of hiding he seems fearless as he confronts Ahab. (1 Kings 20:7-19.) So why do you think he ran away after the contest on Matthew Carmel?

5. What does this tell you about Jezebel's power?

The rest of the story:

We see a little more of the character of Ahab and Jezebel in a later account. Their palace looked out on the vineyard of a godly Israelite named Naboth. Ahab envied his neighbor's prosperous vineyard and finally offered to buy it from him. But Naboth knew he had a God-given right to keep property in his family, so he refused to sell it. Ahab's response was to pout, hide out in his bedroom, and refuse to eat.

When Jezebel heard about it she assured him she would get the vineyard for him. And she did. She proclaimed a feast in Naboth's town. Then she hired a couple of scoundrels (that's what the Bible calls them) to lie and accuse Naboth of blasphemy. The punishment for blasphemy was stoning, so Naboth was executed and his land reverted to the king.

The news of Naboth's death got Ahab back on his feet. But while he surveyed his new vineyard, Elijah the Prophet appeared and warned him he would not live to enjoy his new acquisition and that Jezebel would die and be eaten by dogs in Jezreel – site of their seasonal palace.

Not long after, Ahab led his troops in battle, disguising himself so that the enemy would think someone else was the leader. However, God knew exactly where he was, and God directed a "random" arrow to take Ahab's life.

Jezebel lived another ten years. Their son Ahaziah continued their godless reign in Israel, probably still under much direction from Jezebel. Ten years after Elijah's prophesy, Jehu led a revolt in Israel, and Jezebel's evil life ended as violently as it had been lived.

When Jehu came to the palace tower in Jezreel, Jezebel seemed to know her end was near. To prepare, she put on her make-up and had her hair done in a queenly style. Then she greeted Jehu with a shouted insult from the tower window.

Jehu's answer was to direct her servants to throw her down, which they were quick to do. The Bible tells us her blood was spattered on the walls and, when Jehu later sent servants out to bury her body, all they could find were her skull, her feet, and the palms of her hands. The predicted dogs had done their gruesome work.

What's in it for me?

No one would want to imagine they could be as evil as Jezebel. You won't find little girls carrying her name. However, each of us is capable of evil. Any hint of "my-way-or-the-highway" or manipulation to get our own way should alert our hearts to their selfish tendencies.

Application:

1. What good qualities did Jezebel possess?

2. What caused her to be so evil?

3. Did she have opportunities to repent? When (or where)?

4. Why do you think she stopped pursuing Elijah?

5. Why do you think her life ended so violently?

6. What do you personally take from Jezebel for your own life?

7. Write a title for this lesson on Jezebel.

Response:

Has something from this study of Jezebel touched your
life? Take a minute and write your prayer of response to
God.

For Further Study:
1 Kings 16:31-33; 18:20-40; 19:1-10; 21:1-28; 2 Kings
9:30-37.

Esther: _____

Just Imagine

Motherless – fatherless – a Jewess in a foreign land, part of a subject people. What would your fate be? You are four generations removed from your homeland and, although the Persian kings have allowed Jews to return to Judah, your guardian, cousin Mordecai, has not elected to go that way. Maybe the fact that he has a good civil service job keeps him in Persia.

Or maybe it's because he has undertaken your care, for he treats you as a father would. Your only hope will be to convince him to find you the most prosperous young Jewish man available.

Mordecai is at the king's court daily. He brings home all the news. Last year Persia won a great war and King Ahasuerus celebrated with a six-month long drinking party. It's a good thing he had men like Mordecai to keep his business affairs in order. The party ended with Ahasuerus' queen being deposed because she wouldn't show off her charms for the king's drinking buddies. She was a brave woman. But she lost her place as queen.

Now the king has decided he needs a new queen. Mordecai says he's really supposed to choose a woman from one of seven royal families, but he's bypassing that rule. He's following the advice of his drunken advisors and rounding up all the young virgins in the kingdom.

And you're one of them. What are your thoughts, hopes, and fears?

Read All About Esther:

Esther 2:1) After these things, when the wrath of King Ahasuerus subsided, he remembered Vashti, what she had done, and what had been decreed against her. 2) Then the king's servants who attended him said: "Let beautiful young virgins be sought for the king; 3) "and let the king appoint officers in all the provinces of his kingdom that they may gather all the beautiful young virgins to Shushan the citadel, into the women's quarters, under the custody of Hegai the king's eunuch, custodian of the women. And let beauty preparations be given them. 4) "Then let the young woman who pleases the king be queen instead of Vashti."

This thing pleased the king, and he did so.

5) In Shushan the citadel there was a certain Jew whose name was Mordecai the son of Jair, the son of Shimei, the son of Kish, a Benjamite. 6) Kish having been carried away from Jerusalem with the captives who had been captured with Jeconiah king of Judah, whom Nebuchadnezzar the king of Babylon had carried away. 7) And Mordecai had brought up Hadassah, that is, Esther, his uncle's daughter, for she had neither father nor mother. The young woman was lovely and beautiful. When her father and mother died, Mordecai took her as his own daughter.

8) So it was, when the king's command and decree were heard, and when many young women were gathered at Shushan the citadel, under the custody of Hegai, that Esther also was taken to the king's palace, into the care of Hegai the custodian of the women. 9) Now the young woman pleased him, and she obtained his favor; so he readily gave beauty preparations to her, besides her allowance. Then seven choice maidservants were provided for her from the king's palace, and he moved her and her maidservants to the best place in the house of the women.

10) Esther had not revealed her people or family, for Mordecai had charged her not to reveal it. 11) And every day Mordecai paced in front of the court of the women's quarters, to learn of Esther's welfare and what was happening to her.

12) Each young woman's turn came to go in to King Ahasuerus after she had completed twelve months' preparation, according to the regulations for the women,

*for thus were the days of their preparation apportioned: six
months with oil of myrrh, and six months with perfumes
and preparations for beautifying women. 13) Thus
prepared, each young woman went to the king, and she was
given whatever she desired to take with her from the
women's quarters to the king's palace. 14) In the evening
she went, and in the morning she returned to the second
house of the women, to the custody of Shaashgaz, the king's
eunuch who kept the concubines. She would not go in to the
king again unless the king delighted in her and called for
her by name.*

*15) Now when the turn came for Esther the daughter of
Abihail the uncle of Mordecai , who had taken her as his
daughter, to go in to the king, she requested nothing but
what Hegai the king's eunuch, the custodian of the women,
advised. And Esther obtained favor in the sight of all who
saw her. 16) So Esther was taken to King Ahasuerus, into
his royal palace, in the tenth month, which is the month of
Tebeth, in the seventh year of his reign.*

*17) The king loved Esther more than all the other women,
and she obtained grace and favor in his sight, more than all
the virgins; so he set the royal crown upon her head and
made her queen instead of Vashti. 18) Then the king made
a great feast, the Feast of Esther, for all his officials and
servants; and he proclaimed a holiday in the provinces and
gave gifts according to the generosity of a king.*

Any questions?

Clarifications:

Hadassah – myrtle (her Jewish name)

Esther – star (her Persian name)

Mordecai – 4th generation from dispersion under Nebuchadnezzar; Benjamite; probably a civil servant under Xerxes

Ahasuerus -- known as Xerxes in secular writings; son of Darius I

Haman – Prime Minister under Xerxes; descendant of Agag, one of the kings conquered by Joshua

Shushan – capital city of Persia, now Iran.

Let's think about it.

Chapter 1 of Esther sets the scene. Read it to learn about the characters involved.

1. Describe Xerxes (Ahasuerus).

2. Describe Vashti.

Chapter 2 adds Esther and Mordecai.

3. Describe Esther.

4. Describe Mordecai.

5. What kind of beauty contest was this?

The rest of the story:

All seemed quiet in the palace. But God placed Esther in her position for a reason. During the first five years of her reign, the only mention we hear of her is when she reported a plot against the king, discovered by her cousin Mordecai.

Then things began to move. First the king promoted Haman to Prime Minister. Haman was a vain man who expected everyone to bow to him after this great honor. Mordecai was the only man who refused to bow. The Bible doesn't tell us why he would not bow, other than the fact that he was a Jew. Apparently, everyone knew that the Jews did not bow to anyone except their God. So Haman vowed to get rid of not just Mordecai, but all of the Jews. He bribed the king to make such a decree. Amazingly, the king did not even know that his own queen was one of Haman's hated people.

When Mordecai heard the decree read, he immediately put on sackcloth, covered himself with ashes, and went about the city loudly decrying their fate. Of course, Esther heard about this, so she sent her servant to find out what terrible thing had caused his actions. Mordecai responded with the request for her to beg the king to counter his edict. His famous words are, "Yet who knows whether you have come to the kingdom for such a time as this?"

Esther was justifiably afraid. Even the queen could not approach Xerxes without being summoned. She had not seen the king for a whole month. If she asked an audience of him and he chose not to receive her, she could very well be executed. But she understood their desperation and agreed to go to the king, after three days of fasting with her maidens and Mordecai's promise to gather the Jews of the city to fast as well. Fasting implies prayer, although it is not directly mentioned.

True to her word, Esther fasted, prayed, and approached Xerxes three days later. The king indicated his pleasure by extending his scepter to her. He knew she was deeply troubled, or she would not have come to him, and he offered to meet her request, up to giving her half of his kingdom.

However, Esther took her time. She invited the king and his prime minister to a banquet. At the dinner, Xerxes again asked her request, and again, she invited them to another banquet the next day.

Meanwhile, proud Haman was so elevated by her special attention that he went home bragging about it. The only bad thing he could see was his nemesis Mordecai, who still did not bow to him. His wife and friends suggested he build a gallows and get the king's permission to impale Mordecai on it. Haman immediately had the gallows built.

That night Xerxes could not sleep. Instead of having his musicians attempt to soothe him, he decided to have the court records read to him. Toward morning they came to the part about Mordecai saving the king's life several years before. Xerxes realized Mordecai had not received a reward for that, so he determined to rectify that omission.

Just then Haman entered the king's bedchamber, wanting to get an early start on his revenge on Mordecai. The king had his own question to ask first: What should he do to greatly honor a deserving subject?

Of course, Haman thought Xerxes must mean himself, so he suggested a parade, setting up the honoree in the king's own robe, seated on the king's own horse, led by a noble prince who would announce the king's honor. Imagine Haman's face when Xerxes told him to be the one to honor Mordecai in this way!

Haman was so upset after carrying out that duty, that he had to be summoned to the palace for Esther's second banquet. This time, when Xerxes asked Esther her request, she told him of the decree against her people and pointed to Haman as the instigator of it. The king's response was to have Haman impaled on the gallows he had prepared for Mordecai, and to have Esther and Mordecai issue a further decree allowing the Jews to defend themselves. He even made Mordecai his new prime minister.

What's in it for me?

The story of Esther is like a grand opera tale, seemingly bigger than life. But God IS bigger than life. If we look back in our own lives, we probably recognize times when He placed us in positions to serve him that took our courage and trust to do so. We were there "for such a time as this." Whenever something we must do causes us to depend totally on God, we can consider it an Esther event.

Application:

1. God's name is not mentioned in the Book of Esther. Why might that be? What evidence is there that He is in charge anyway?

2. What might have happened if Esther had not responded to Mordecai's request to go to the king?

3. What gave Esther the courage to go to the king?

4.How do you recognize an "Esther event?" How do you respond to that?

5. What do you personally take away from Esther for your own life?

6. Write an appropriate title for this lesson on Esther.

Response:

Has something from this study of Esther touched your life? Take a minute and write your prayer of response to God.

For Further Study:
Esther, chapters 1 through 10.

Mary (of Nazareth): __

<u>***Just Imagine***</u>

OK – this time let's not imagine. Let's think about what you already know – or think you know -- about Mary, this woman who has appeared in more paintings than any other woman in all history, and about whom much tradition is written. What was she like?

<u>***Read All About Mary:***</u>

Luke 1:26) Now in the sixth month the angel Gabriel was sent by God to a city of Galilee named Nazareth, 27) to a virgin betrothed to a man whose name was Joseph, of the

house of David. The virgin's name was Mary. 28) And having come in, the angel said to her, "Rejoice, highly favored one, the Lord is with you; blessed are you among women!"

29) But when she saw him, she was troubled at his saying, and considered what manner of greeting this was. 30) Then the angel said to her, "Do not be afraid, Mary, for you have found favor with God. 31) "And behold, you will conceive in your womb and bring forth a Son, and shall call His name Jesus. 32) "He will be great, and will be called the Son of the Highest; and the Lord God will give Him the throne of His father David. 33) "And He will reign over the house of Jacob forever, and of His kingdom there will be no end."

34) Then Mary said to the angel, "How can this be, since I do not know a man?"

35) And the angel answered and said to her, "The Holy Spirit will come upon you, and the power of the Highest will overshadow you; therefore, also, that Holy One who is to be born will be called the Son of God. 36) "Now indeed, Elizabeth your relative has also conceived a son in her old age; and this is now the sixth month for her who was called barren. 37) "For with God nothing will be impossible."

38) Then Mary said, "Behold the maidservant of the Lord! Let it be to me according to your word."

And the angel departed from her.

39) Now Mary arose in those days and went into the hill country with haste, to a city of Judah, 40) and entered the house of Zacharias and greeted Elizabeth. 41) And it happened, when Elizabeth heard the greeting of Mary, that the babe leaped in her womb; and Elizabeth was filled with the Holy Spirit. 42) Then she spoke out with a loud voice and said, "Blessed are you among women, and blessed is the fruit of your womb! 43) "But why is this granted to me, that the mother of my Lord should come to me? 44) "For indeed, as soon as the voice of your greeting sounded in my ears, the babe leaped in my womb for joy. 45) "Blessed is she who believed, for there will be a fulfillment of those things which were told her from the Lord."

46) And Mary said:
        "My soul magnifies the Lord,
47) And my spirit has rejoiced in God my Savior.

Any questions?

Clarifications:

1. What do we know about Mary from the passage just read?

2. What do we not know?

Let's think about it.

Let's go on with Mary's story.

3. What does Mary's song tell us about her relationship to God? (Luke 1:46-55)

4. What do we learn about her in Luke 2:1-7?

5. What new facts come from Luke 2:8-20?

6. What happened next (and when)? (Luke 2:21)

7. Next? (Luke 2:22-38) (Lev. 12:2-8)

8. Then Luke says they returned to Nazareth, but he left out part of the story. What's missing? (Matthew 2)

9. Where is Joseph in all of this?

The rest of the story:

What else do you know about Mary? Can you imagine raising a perfect son? We don't know how long the family remained in Egypt, but Jesus was a young child, and Mary and Joseph had begun their family that eventually included James, Joses, Simeon, Judas and their sisters.

We next find Mary mentioned in Luke 2:41-51. By the time Jesus was twelve years old he realized God was his Father, biologically as well as spiritually, the way many Jews knew him to be. The family's annual temple visit gave him the opportunity to learn even more about God than Mary, Joseph and the Nazareth rabbis taught him. At twelve, Jewish boys are considered men. This is why He was included in the annual trek to Jerusalem.

The Bible says Mary and Joseph did not understand his statement that he must be about his Father's business – but Mary, as usual, treasured all this in her heart.

Somewhere between Jesus' twelfth birthday and his thirtieth, Joseph apparently died. Tradition says he was considerably older than Mary. Jesus must have taken over the family business of carpentry, then passed it on to his brothers when it came time for him to present himself as the Messiah to Israel. As we read through the Gospels, we can imagine places where Mary might have been on the sidelines.

We know where Mary was at his first miracle, for it was she who brought the lack of wine to Jesus' attention. We do not know of any other miracle he had done before then, but Mary was confident of his ability to take care of the situation. They had doubtless talked about his mission, for he reminded her that it was not yet his "hour." She instructed the servants to do as he said and Jesus turned the water into wine.

She was with Jesus at the beginning of his ministry. We further read of a group of women who followed Jesus and his disciples in order to minister to their physical needs. Later we find her and her other sons asking to see him – concerned about his safety or his sanity – during his travels. His response was to remind her and all listeners that he must consider his followers the same as his family.

Remember Simeon's prophecy? Surely Mary remembered as Jesus' ministry became more and more controversial. Imagine her mother's heart at the triumphal entry and the ensuing harassment from the scribes and priests. Think how she must have wanted to stay close to Him during that next week, which culminated in the crucifixion.

We find her at the foot of the cross. Her Son, the Messiah, had not forgotten her even there. He remanded her into the care of his beloved disciple, John. She later helped make John's house a gathering place for Christians.

She was among the women who found the tomb empty that first Resurrection Sunday.
It was not until after the resurrection that her other children trusted Him as their Messiah, but her heart must have overflowed as each one came to Him for salvation.

That's all we know about Mary, and that's probably more than she would want us to know. Jesus Christ was her son, but also her Savior. She wanted the attention on him.

What's in it for me?

Mary's life was filled with the usual highs and lows we all face, except her highs were much higher and her lows exceedingly low. I am impressed with the repeated statement concerning her: "Mary kept all these things in her heart." She saved up the good times. She pondered the prophecies. Surely this habit kept her in touch with God so that she could weather storms that were more intense than any we will have to face.

Application:

It's never too late to work on our relationship to God. The more time we invest in reading His word and talking to Him, inviting Him into every corner of our lives, the more we learn of His loving heart and sustaining power.

1. In what ways are you like Mary?

2. In what ways are you not like Mary? (The real Mary –
not the traditional stories that are not in the Bible.)

3. What from Mary's life encourages you?

4.How can you encourage a Marylike attitude in the
younger people in your life?

5.What do you personally take away from Mary for your
own life?

6. Write an appropriate title for this lesson.

Response:
Has something from this study of Mary touched your life?
Take a minute and write your prayer of response to God.

For Further Study:
Matthew 1:16-20; 2:11; 13:55; Mark 6:3; Luke 1:27-46, 56;
2: 5, 16-19, 34; Acts 1:14.

Elizabeth: _____

Just Imagine

You're past thinking of yourself as a late-day Sarah, even though you are not quite as old as she was when Isaac was born. You've prayed for a child for decades, since your wedding day. You don't understand why God would withhold this joy from you, for you have maintained a godly life, all that is required of the wife of a priest.

Your husband has returned from his temple service and he cannot speak. On the wax writing tablet he writes, "God says we will have a son."

What are your thoughts?

Read All About Elizabeth:

Luke 1:5) There was in the days of Herod, the king of Judea, a certain priest named Zacharias, of the division of Abijah. His wife was of the daughters of Aaron, and her name was Elizabeth. (6) And they were both righteous before God, walking in all the commandments and ordinances of the Lord blameless. (7) But they had no child, because Elizabeth was barren, and they were both well advanced in years.

(8) So it was, that while he was serving as priest before God in the order of his division, (9) according to the custom of the priesthood, his lot fell to burn incense when he went into the temple of the Lord. (10) And the while multitude of the people was praying outside at the hour of incense.

(11) Then an angel of the Lord appeared to him, standing on the right side of the altar of incense. (12) And when Zacharias saw him, he was troubled, and fear fell upon him.

(13) But the angel said to him, "Do not be afraid, Zacharias, for your prayer is heard; and your wife Elizabeth will bear you a son, and you shall call his name John. (14) "And you will have joy and gladness, and many will rejoice at his birth. (15) "For he will be great in the sight of the Lord, and shall drink neither wine nor strong drink. He will also be filled with the Holy Spirit, even from his mother's womb. (16) "And he will turn many of the children of Israel to the Lord their God. (17) "He will also go before Him in the spirit and power of Elijah, 'to turn the hearts of the fathers to the children,' and the disobedient to the wisdom of the just, to make ready a people prepared for the Lord."

(18) And Zacharias said to the angel, "How shall I know this? For I am an old man, and my wife is well advanced in years."

(19) And the angel answered and said to him, "I am Gabriel, who stands in the presence of God, and was sent to speak to you and bring you these glad tidings. (20) "But behold, you will be mute and not able to speak until the day these things take place, because you did not believe my words which will be fulfilled in their own time."

(21) And the people waited for Zacharias, and marveled that he lingered so long in the temple. (22) But when he came out, he could not speak to them; and they perceived that he had seen a vision in the temple, for he beckoned to them and remained speechless.

(23) So it was, as soon as the days of his service were completed, that he departed to his own house. (24) Now after those days his wife Elizabeth conceived; and she hid herself five months, saying, (25) Thus the Lord has dealt with me, in the days when He looked on me, to take away my reproach among people."

Any questions?

Clarifications:

Elizabeth – means "God is my oath." Hebrew form of the word is Elisheba, also the name of the first priest, Aaron's, wife

Zacharias – means "Yahweh remembers"

John – means "mercy or favor of God."

Zacharias and Elizabeth lived in the **Judean hills**, in a little town (possibly Ain Karim) about four miles north of Jerusalem.

Priests served at the temple for six-month periods of time. During his tour of duty, Zacharias had the honor of burning incense in the sanctuary. This great honor would only be conferred on a priest once in his life – if ever.

Let's think about it.

1. What kind of woman was Elizabeth? (Leviticus 21:7)

2. What kind of man was her husband, Zacharias?

3. Luke 1:6 says they were "blameless." What does that mean?

4. How was Elizabeth's life like Sarah's?

5. How was her life different than Sarah's?

6. Why do you think she hid instead of announcing her pregnancy to her community?

7. What did she mean by her "reproach?"

The rest of the story:

Elizabeth's pregnancy was just the first miracle she experienced. For whatever reason, she decided not to share her good news with her community. Then in her sixth month she had a surprise visit from her young cousin, Mary.

Luke 2:41) And it happened, when Elizabeth heard the greeting of Mary, that the babe leaped in her womb; and Elizabeth was filled with the Holy Spirit. (42) Then she spoke out with a loud voice and said, "Blessed are you among women, and blessed is the fruit of your womb! 43) "But why is this granted to me, that the mother of my Lord should come to me? 44) "For indeed, as soon as the voice of your greeting sounded in my ears, the babe leaped in my womb for joy. 45) "Blessed is she who believed, for there will be a fulfillment of those things which were told her from the Lord."

Imagine the bonding between these two women in the three months Mary visited. Surely they pored over the prophecies that involved the babes they carried.

Shortly after Mary returned to Nazareth, Elizabeth went into labor and brought forth the son Zacharias had been promised. True to the letter of the law, friends and family gathered for the child's circumcision and naming. They expected him to be named after his father, but Elizabeth said, "No, his name is John." When they argued with her that there was no one in her family by that name, she stood her ground.

So they appealed to Zacharias. As soon as he wrote, "His name is John" on the tablet, his tongue was freed and he could speak again. His first words glorified God and prophesied John's life.

The neighbors went away, shaking their heads, asking, "What kind of child will this be?"

Zacharias' prophecy at John's circumcision said he would be called the prophet of the Highest, and go before Him to prepare His way and prepare the people for the knowledge of salvation.

Elizabeth and Zacharias taught John well, for the Bible says he grew and became strong in spirit. He must have learned to find his strength in solitude with God, for he made his home in the deserts until he began his ministry of preaching repentance and preparation for Jesus' coming.

Could it be that God left Elizabeth childless until late in life so that she would not be alive to see the atrocities faced by her beloved son?

What's in it for me?

Childlessness is a difficult burden. Today we have medical advances that help many couples conceive. Neither Sarah nor Elizabeth had those options. They were totally dependent on the Lord. (We still are, but we sometimes forget that.) Sarah stepped out of God's will and brought sorrow to the world – trouble that continues today.

Elizabeth simply waited on God and would have gone childless to her grave if that were God's will.

In the Jewish economy, children were considered evidence of God's blessing on a family. The reverse was equally true: childlessness was considered an evidence of God's judgment. Elizabeth bore this unjust criticism – probably only implied behind her back, but real, none-the-less.

Beyond the reproach is the issue of loneliness. The childless, quiet household is a lonely place. Sometimes the lonely woman is one who has raised her children and they have moved away. She longs for companionship and interaction with little people again.

Think of ways to reach out to lonely people, maybe even sharing your grandchildren with those who have none, or at least none who live nearby.

Application:

1. What indications are there that Elizabeth was a good wife?

2. What indications are there that Elizabeth was a good mother? (Matthew 11:7-19)

3.What fruit of the Spirit do you see in her life? (Galatians 5:22-23)

4.What do you personally take away from Elizabeth for your own life?

5. Write an appropriate title for this lesson on Elizabeth.

Response:

Has something from this study of Elizabeth touched your life? Take a minute and write your prayer of response to God.

For Further Study:
Luke 1:5-20, 24-25, 39-45; Matthew 3:1-17; 11:1-19; 14:1-13.

Mary & Martha: _____

Just Imagine

We're all a combination of Mary and Martha, but we lean to one personality or the other. Are you more of a doer, like Martha? Or more of a quiet responder, like Mary? Why do you think so?

Read All About Mary and Martha:

Luke 10:38) Now it happened as they went that He entered a certain village, and a certain woman named Martha welcomed Him into her house. 39) And she had a sister called Mary, who also sat at Jesus' feet and heard His word.

40) But Martha was distracted with much serving, and she approached Him and said, "Lord, do You not care that my sister has left me to serve alone? Therefore tell her to help me."

41) And Jesus answered and said to her, "Martha, Martha, you are worried and troubled about many things, 42) "But one thing is needed, and Mary has chosen that good part, which will not be taken away from her."

Any questions?

Clarifications:

Bethany – a village two miles east or Jerusalem.

Lazarus – Mary and Martha's brother; apparently the three siblings shared a home

Simon – another resident of Bethany, a Pharisee who invited Jesus into his home

Let's think about it.

1. Describe Martha.

2. Have you known any Marthas? What do you think made them so bossy?

3. Describe Mary.

4. Have you known any Marys? What do you think made them learners?

5. A contributing factor to Mary's love for Jesus is found in John 12:1-8. The story is similar to that in Luke 11:26-50, but the woman is not named so we don't know for sure that it is Mary's story. However, it happens at about the same time and in the same home (Simon's) as the other accounts of Mary anointing Jesus with costly perfume, so it could be the same instance. What would cause Mary to love Jesus so much that she would pour perfume (worth a year's wages) on his head and/or feet?

The rest of the story:

Jesus must have spent a lot of time with Lazarus' family.
He loved each of them. One day, near the end of his time of
ministry, he received news that Lazarus was deathly ill.
Jesus had incurred enemies in the Jerusalem area, so I'm
sure the disciples wondered what he would do about the
news.

Jesus waited. For two more days. Then he said, "Come on.
We're going to Judea."

Thomas (don't you just identify with him?) said, "OK.
Let's go die with Him."

He was sure they would all be executed if they returned to
Jerusalem.

So they went back to Lazarus' home in Bethany, and found
that Lazarus had already died. Now Jesus knew all that
from the beginning.

Let's pick up the story when He arrives at Mary and
Martha's home:

*John 11:20) Then Martha, as soon as she heard that Jesus
was coming, went and met Him, but Mary was sitting in the
house. 21) Now Martha said to Jesus, "Lord, if You had
been here, my brother would not have died. 22) "But even
now I know that whatever You ask of God, God will give
You."*

23) Jesus said to her, "Your brother will rise again."

24) Martha said to Him, "I know that he will rise again in the resurrection at the last day."

25) Jesus said to her, "I am the resurrection and the life. He who believes in Me, though he may die, he shall live. 26) "And whoever lives and believes in Me shall never die. Do you believe this?" 27) She said to Him, "Yes, Lord, I believe that You are the Christ, the Son of God, who is to come into the world."

28) And when she had said these things, she went her way and secretly called Mary her sister, saying, "The Teacher has come and is calling for you."

29) As soon as she heard that, she arose quickly and came to Him. 30) Now Jesus had not yet come into the town, but was in the place where Martha met Him. 31) Then the Jews who were with her in the house, and comforting her, when they saw that Mary rose up quickly and went out, followed her, saying, "She is going to the tomb to weep there."

32) Then, when Mary came where Jesus was, and saw Him, she fell down at His feet, saying to Him, "Lord, if You had been here, my brother would not have died."

33) Therefore, when Jesus saw her weeping, and the Jews who came with her weeping, He groaned in the spirit and was troubled. 34) And He said, "Where have you laid him?" They said to Him, "Come and see."

35) Jesus wept.

We know the rest of the story. Jesus proved His power over death by raising Lazarus from the grave.

What's in it for me?

Whether we are more like Mary or Martha, we all go through difficult times. We all have sin to confess and forsake. We all have our reasons for loving our Lord Jesus.

Application:

1. In the story of Lazarus' resurrection, where do we find Martha?

2 Where do we find Mary?

3. Which sister states her faith in Jesus' resurrection power?

4. Which sister berates the Lord for not answering sooner?

5. Why do you think Jesus wept?

6. Are you more of a Mary or a Martha?

7.What's missing in your Mary/Martha balance?

8. What can you do to achieve more of a balance (or what have you done in this regard)?

9. What do you personally take away from Mary and Martha for your own life?

10. Write an appropriate title for this lesson on Mary and Martha.

Response:
Has something from this study of Mary and Martha touched your life? Take a minute and write your prayer of response to God.

For further study:
Matthew 26:6-13; Mark 14:3-9; Luke 7:36-50; 10:38-42; John 11:1-44; 12: 1-11.

Mary Magdalene: _ _ _ _

Just Imagine

You are a businesswoman in the prosperous town of
Magdala, doing well but afraid of losing your inherited
holdings because of recurring demonic attacks. Some days
you are clear headed and able to make necessary decisions.
Other days you feel you are going out of your mind.
Demonic activity is not all that unusual, but your pact with
the devil has not brought you relief.

Then you hear of a young rabbi who is traveling in the
nearby government center of Capernaum. It is said he has
cast out demons and healed all matter of illnesses.

You wonder --

Read All About Mary Magdalene:

*Luke 8:1) Now it came to pass, afterward, that He went
through every city and village, preaching and bringing the*

glad tidings of the kingdom of God. And the twelve were with Him, 2) and certain women who had been healed of evil spirits and infirmities – Mary called Magdalene, out of whom had come seven demons, 3) and Joanna the wife of Chuza, Herod's steward, and Susanna, and many others who provided for Him from their substance.

Any questions?

Clarifications:

Another Mary – probably the most common name in the Bible, at least for women. Remember from the study of Ruth that it means "bitter."

Magdalene – from Magdala, which means "tower" or "castle" and was a large, thriving town on the coast of Galilee about three miles from Capernaum. It was known for dye works and primitive textile factories. Mary apparently had enough money to allow her to donate to the Lord's earthly ministry, and enough free time to accompany the group.

Let's think about it.

1. Was Mary afflicted with demons or just a mental illness?

2. Look up "demons, demonic" in a concordance. How many instances do you find recorded of demonic activity?

3. Why do you think there was so much demonic activity when Jesus was on earth?

4. Is there demonic activity on earth today?

5. What was Mary's response to being freed from the demons?

6. Who were the women who traveled with Jesus and His disciples?

7. How did the women serve the disciples?

The rest of the story:

It seems that Jesus cast the demons out of Mary Magdalene early in His ministry. For the rest of his travels she apparently led a group of women (indicated because her name usually comes first) in taking care of the disciples, particularly their meals. We do not read of her specifically again until we find her at the foot of the cross.

Surely she was there at the last supper and probably followed the eleven and Jesus out to the Garden of Gethsemane. She may have been right there when Jesus was arrested. She is mentioned the next day at the foot of the cross with His mother Mary and James' and John's mother. Matthew mentions that she sat outside the tomb. Did she spend the night there? Maybe.

The third day we find her, early in the morning, coming with spices to properly care for Jesus' body. Let me tell you about that in a poem.

GARDENS

A garden is a lovely place,
Its fragrance fills the air.
My Lord was in a garden
When He agonized in prayer.

In the quiet of a garden
As you come apart to pray
Be reminded of a Savior
Who wept alone that day.

The tomb was in a garden,
That borrowed place of rest;
And Joseph must have marveled
That his place should be so blest.

Mary asked the "gardener,"
As she wandered, weeping, there,
If the body of her Master
Was entrusted to his care.

But "Mary!" was the word He spoke,
And "Master!" her reply.
Oh, what joy now filled the garden
And her heart at that glad cry!

God planned this happy season,
When gardens start to bloom,
To bring to our remembrance
That garden's empty tomb!

D. Saunders

She must have fallen to her knees at His feet, but He cautioned her not to touch Him, but to go tell His disciples to meet Him in Galilee. Can you imagine the wild abandon of this woman racing to the upper room to give His message to them?

What's in it for me?

1. What has Jesus cast out of your life?

2. What changes has Jesus brought to your life?

3. How do you show your love for the Savior?

4. Imagine the bravery involved in following Jesus all the way to the cross. What would it take to make you that brave?

5. Imagine the sorrow and disappointment of seeing the one you thought to be the Messiah crucified. Why do you think Mary still stayed by the tomb in spite of this?

6. Why do you think Mary did not recognize Jesus in the garden?

7. How does our sadness sometimes keep up from seeing recognizing Jesus in our circumstances?

8. We don't read anything more about Mary Magdalene after the Gospels, but where do you think she would be on the day of Pentecost?

9. What do you personally take away from Mary Magdalene for your own life?

10. Write an appropriate title for this lesson on Mary Magdalene.

Application:

In a sense, Mary was the first missionary: the first to bear the good news of Jesus' resurrection. She was not afraid to tell what she knew. We may not have had seven demons cast out of us, but Jesus can and will meet all of our needs with forgiveness, healing, and provision, just as He did Mary Magdalene. We can enjoy that same closeness with the risen Savior that Mary did. We can tell the world what He's done for us and what He will do for any who come to Him – just as she did.

Response:

Has something from this study of Mary Magdalene touched your life? Take a minute and write your prayer of response to God.

For Further Study:
Matthew 27: 56, 61; 28:1; Mark 15:40, 47; 16:1-19; Luke 8:2; 24:10; John 19:25; 20:1-18.

Dorcas: _____

Just Imagine

The love of your life has lost his life in a storm at sea. You are left with two young children and no way to earn an income. Fortunately, God has brought you to a group of Jesus' followers who pool their resources and help with food. Best of all, another believer, who is a gifted seamstress, has undertaken to keep you and your children clothed.

How do you feel about this woman?

What would you do for her?

What might be your worries about her?

Read All About Dorcas:

Acts 9:36) At Joppa there was a certain disciple named Tabitha, which is translated Dorcas. This woman was full of good works and charitable deeds which she did.

37) But it happened in those days that she became sick and died. When they had washed her, they laid her in an upper room.38) And since Lydda was near Joppa, and the disciples had heard that Peter was there, they sent two men to him, imploring him not to delay in coming to them.

39) Then Peter arose and went with them. When he had come, they brought him to the upper room. And all the widows stood by him weeping, showing the tunics and garments which Dorcas had made while she was with them.

40) But Peter put them all out, and knelt down and prayed. And turning to the body he said, "Tabitha, arise."

And she opened her eyes, and when she saw Peter she sat up. 41) Then he gave her his hand and lifted her up; and when he had called the saints and widows, he presented her alive.

42) And it became known throughout all Joppa, and many believed on the Lord.

43) So it was that he stayed many days in Joppa with Simon, a tanner.

Any questions?

Clarifications:

Dorcas – means gazelle. Hebrew form is Tabitha.

Joppa – seaport town on the Mediterranean, 34 miles northwest of Jerusalem

Let's think about it.

1. Dorcas is called a "disciple." Explain that.

2. In contrast – what is an apostle?

3. What do we know about Dorcas?

4. What do we not know?

5. Who was at her "funeral?"

6. What did they show Peter?

7. Why would the disciples of Joppa send for Peter after Dorcas died?

8. How did Peter know what to do for Dorcas (and her mourners)? (Mark 5:22-24, 35-42)

9. What did Peter do after raising Dorcas from the dead?

The rest of the story:

Romans 12:1)*I beseech you therefore, brethren, by the mercies of God, that you present your bodies a living sacrifice, holy, acceptable to God, which is your reasonable service. 2) And do not be conformed to this world, but be transformed by the renewing of you mind, that you may prove what is that good and acceptable and perfect will of God.*

3) For I say, through the grace given to me, to everyone who is among you, not to think of himself more highly than he ought to think, but to think soberly, as God has dealt to each one a measure of faith.

4) For as we have many members in one body, but all the members do not have the same function, 5) so we, being many, are one body in Christ, and individually members of one another.

6) Having then gifts differing according to the grace that is given to us, let us use them: if prophecy, let us prophesy in proportion to our faith; 7) or ministry, let us use it in our ministering; he who teaches, in teaching; 8) he who exhorts, in exhortation; he who gives, with liberality; he who leads, with diligence; he who shows mercy, with cheerfulness.

What's in it for me?

1. What was Dorcas' spiritual gift?

2. How did she use it?

3. What gifts do I have?

4. How do I use them to serve my Lord?

5. Is there some gift I am neglecting?

6.What do you personally take away from Dorcas for your own life?

7.Write an appropriate title for the lesson on Dorcas.

Application:

The story of Dorcas comes early in the New Testament church. It's the chapter after Saul's conversion and comes before Peter is arrested in Jerusalem. It is before Paul and Barnabus began their missionary trips, so the fact that there were already believers in towns like Joppa lets us know the apostles had already begun to spread the Gospel, particularly as they scattered from the persecution that centered in Jerusalem. Dorcas, like us, came to believe in Jesus because of someone else's testimony. I don't know who taught her, but she obviously understood the gift of helps. No other gift is mentioned in her life, but she used what she had to the greatest advantage she could. What an example to us!

173

Response:

Has God touched your heart or taught you something new
as you have studied about
Dorcas? Write your prayer of response to Him.

For Further Study:
Acts 9:36-43; Romans 12:4-8; James 1:27

Priscilla: _____

Just Imagine

Imagine the freedom of a Roman woman living in New Testament times. You are the modern workingwoman who has it all. You run your household, help your husband in the family business, and enjoy learning about all the new events, inventions and philosophies of the capital city. You relish evenings of discussing with your husband what you hear in the shop during the day. Being Jewish, he enjoys bantering with you, so that he encourages you to stretch your mind and learn. In Roman households only the men are so privileged.

In your contacts with Rome's world travelers and emissaries, you learn of a new religion – better known as The Way. Your study brings you to acceptance that Jesus is the Messiah – the Christ -- foretold in the Torah, and you and your husband seek to learn more and more about The Way. You just wish more of your people would see this truth.

You hear that Jesus' followers are called Christians in some parts of the Roman world.

Then disaster strikes. Because of all the controversy about the One Emperor Claudius calls Chrestus, all Jews are expelled from Rome. Only fleetingly do you entertain the thought that you might avoid the expulsion. But no. Everyone knows you and Aquila are Jews and Christians.

So you and Aquila pack up your business and flee to Corinth. What are your thoughts and plans as you travel?

Read All About Priscilla:

Acts 18:11) After these things Paul departed from Athens and went to Corinth. 2) And he found a certain Jew named Aquila, born in Pontus, who had recently come from Italy with his wife Priscilla (because Claudius had commanded all the Jews to depart from Rome); and he came to them.

3) So, because he was of the same trade, he stayed with them and worked; for by occupation they were tentmakers. 4) And he reasoned in the synagogue every Sabbath, and persuaded both Jews and Greeks.
5) When Silas and Timothy had come from Macedonia, Paul was compelled by the Spirit, and testified to the Jews that Jesus is the Christ. 6) But when they opposed him and blasphemed, he shook his garments and said to them, "Your blood be upon your own heads; I am clean. From now on I will go to the Gentiles."

7) And he departed from there and entered the house of a certain man named Justus, one who worshiped God, whose house was next door to the synagogue. 8) Then Crispus, the ruler of the synagogue, believed on the Lord with all his household. And many of the Corinthians, hearing, believed and were baptized.

9) Now the Lord spoke to Paul in the night by a vision, "Do not be afraid, but speak, and do not keep silent; 10) For I am with you, and no one will attack you to hurt you; for I have many people in this city."

11) And he continued there a year and six months, teaching the word of God among them.

12) When Gallio was proconsul of Achaia, the Jews, with one accord rose up against Paul and brought him to the judgment seat. 13) saying, "This fellow persuades men to worship God contrary to the law."

14) And when Paul was about to open his mouth, Gallio said to the Jews, "If it were a matter of wrongdoing or wicked crimes, O Jews, there would be reason why I should bear with you. 15) But if it is a question of words and names and your own law, look to it yourselves; for I do not want to be a judge of such matters."

16) And he drove them from the judgment seat. 17) Then all the Greeks took Sosthenes, the ruler of the synagogue, and beat him before the judgment seat. But Gallio took no notice of these things.

18) So Paul still remained a good while. Then he took leave of the brethren and sailed for Syria, and Priscilla and

Aquila were with him. He had his hair cut off at Cenchrea, for he had taken a vow. 19) And he came to Ephesus, and left them there; but he himself entered the synagogue and reasoned with the Jews. 20) When they asked him to stay a longer time with them, he did not consent, 21) but took leave of them, saying, "I must by all means keep this coming feast in Jerusalem; but I will return again to you, God willing."

And he sailed from Ephesus. 22) And when he had landed at Caesare,. and gone up and greeted the church, he went down to Antioch. 23) After he had spent some time there, he departed and went over the region of Galatia and Phrygia in order, strengthening all the disciples.

Any questions?

Clarifications:

Pontus – Greek community on the southern coast of the Black Sea

Priscilla and Aquila – Greek names, but probably Jewish because they were part of the expulsion from Rome. The fact that Priscilla's name is first in four of their six mentions indicates her prominence. She may have been the more scholarly or maybe the first to believe. She might have even been the one to lead her husband to Christ.

Ephesus – site of one of the major missionary churches. Commended by Christ in Revelation 2:1-7.

Let's think about it.

1. What do we know about Priscilla?

2. What do we not know?

3. What would be involved in tent-making?

4. What does this tell us about Paul?

5. Trace Priscilla and Aquila's moves. What did they do in each of these places?

Acts 18:1 –

Acts 18:18-19 –

Romans 16:3-5 –

2 Timothy 4:19 –

6. Paul says they risked their lives for his sake (Romans 16:3-4). When might that have been? (Acts 19:20-41)

The rest of the story:

Priscilla lived in desperate times, particularly for
Christians. Where the Gospel had been preached there was
already enough controversy that the emperor banned the
Jews from his capital. In other places, such as Ephesus, the
Jews considered it blasphemy and the Greeks thought Jesus
was just another god to add to the many they already
worshiped. Besides that, throughout the Roman Empire,
everyone was expected to worship the emperor himself.

So they followed Paul to Ephesus and were part of the
pioneer church there, providing a meeting place for the
disciples. It was there they met Apollos, a new believer
who came excitedly preaching that the Messiah would be
coming soon. Apparently Jews traveling throughout the
empire had spread that news, because Paul dealt with this
incomplete knowledge in Ephesus as well (Acts 19:1-7).

Priscilla invited this eloquent evangelist into their home
and gently instructed him in the basics of Christianity – that
Christ had already come, lived an exemplary life, healed
the sick, raised the dead, and died on a cruel Roman cross
to pay the penalty for their sins. The best news of all was
that He had risen from the dead to prove He was the
Messiah and that the payment for sin had been accepted.

Apollos traveled on to spread the complete Gospel
throughout Asia Minor. Paul mentioned him in his first
letter to the Corinthians because these ungrounded
believers had divided into factions arguing over who were
the best spiritual leaders. Was Paul jealous of Apollos'

speaking ability? Apparently not; for he said, "I planted, Apollos watered, but God gave the increase."

After Emperor Claudius died, Priscilla and Aquila moved back to Rome. They probably lived there during Paul's incarceration. No doubt Priscilla would have been one who provided his meals or organized women to take care of that need.

Paul was beheaded in Rome. Tradition says Priscilla and Aquila were also beheaded for their faith. Her name appears on many monuments in Rome. That's not the way I'd want to be remembered, but even in her death she exhibited faith and willingness to follow her Savior wherever He led.

What's in it for me?

Throughout the ages women have thought we can't have much spiritual impact, simply because we are women. There are Scriptural passages that warn against women usurping authority over men. Priscilla is a good example of how a godly woman can have a great and godly influence without getting out of God's proper order.

Application:

1. Priscilla simply used her talents and abilities for God. What do you have to use for Him?

2. How are you using your gifts?

3. Do you need to make any adjustments?

4. What do you personally take away from Priscilla for your own life?

5. Write an appropriate title for this lesson.

Response:

Has Priscilla's story impacted your life in any way? Take a
moment to write your prayer of response to God.

For Further Study:
Acts 18:1-28; Romans 16:3; 1 Corinthians 16:19; 2
Timothy 4:19; Ephesians; Revelation 2:1-7.

Your Story

Just Imagine

We've come to the end of our study of Women of the Bible. Before leaving, let's take a final look and remind ourselves of things we've learned. Did you find yourself in God's Book?

Imagine your story written for all to read like the ones we've examined in our study. What are the highlights of your life that might be mentioned?

What are some of your life's low points that God might use to warn other women?

Read all about you:

John 1:10) He (Jesus) was in the world, and the world was made through Him, and the world did not know Him. 11) He came to His own, and His own did not receive Him. 12) But as many as received Him, to them He gave the right to become children of God, to those who believe on His name. 13) who were born, not of blood, nor of the will of the flesh, nor of the will of man, but of God.

Clarifications:

God says your name is written in heaven if you trust in His Son Jesus Christ for your eternal life. John 3:16 says, *For God so loved the world that He gave His only begotten Son, that whoever believes in Him should not perish but have everlasting life.* The word "believes" in the original Greek actually means to trust completely

Let's think about it:

Women of the Old Testament lived under the hard economy of God's law. Even though there are evidences of some understanding about God's grace (especially in the Psalms), the Israelites carried the burden of trying to please God to win his favor.

The rest of the story:

Whether your personal story is mostly positive or mostly negative, God's grace is available for your eternal destiny. The Apostle Paul wrote in Ephesians 2:8-9: *For by grace are you saved through faith, and that not of yourselves; it is the gift of God, not of works, lest anyone should boast.*

What's in it for me:

If you've finished this study and are not sure of your own relationship with God, your choice is before you. God's Son Jesus, the infinite God/man, came to earth to die on a Roman cross to pay the penalty for your sin and purchase a place in heaven for you.

If you already have a Father/daughter relationship with God, Ephesians 2:10 is for you: *For we are His workmanship, created in Christ Jesus for good works, which God prepared beforehand that we should walk in them.*

Application:

After an earth-shaking event, the Philippian jailer asked the Apostle Paul, "What must I do to be saved?" Paul answered, "Believe on the Lord Jesus Christ and you will be saved." Those words still apply today.

Response:

Take a moment to write your prayer of response to God.

For further study:

Book of John; Book of Romans; more studies on the following briefly mentioned Bible Women.

Briefly Mentioned Bible Women

Cain's wife – Genesis 4:17

Lamech's two wives: Adah and Zillah – Genesis 4:19-24

Noah's wife and daughters-in-law – Genesis 6:10; 7:7, 13; 8:18

Hagar – Genesis 16; 21:8-21

Lot's wife – Genesis 19:12-26

Lot's daughters – Genesis 19: 30-38

Keturah – Genesis 25:1-4; 1 Chronicles 32-33

Esau's wives – Genesis 28: 6-9

Tamar (Judah's daughter-in-law) – Genesis 38

Potiphar's wife – Genesis 39:6-20

Asinath – Genesis 41:50-52

Jochebed – Exodus 2:1-10; 6:20;

Zipporah – Exodus 2:16-22; 4:24-26

Moses' second wife – Numbers 12:1-2

Achsah, Caleb's daughter – Joshua 15:16-19

Deborah – Judges 4-5

Jael – Judges 4:11-22

Jephthah's daughter – Judges 11:30-12:40

Manoah's wife – Judges 13

Samson's wife – Judges 14; 15:1-6

Delilah – Judges 16:1-22

Micah's mother – Judges 17:4

Levite's concubine – Judges 19

Naomi – Ruth 1-4

Orpah – Ruth 1:4-14

Peninnah – 1 Samuel 1:1-7

Phineas' wife – 1 Samuel 4:19-22

Michal – 1 Samuel 18:17-30; 19:8-18; 2 Samuel 3:12-16; 6:16-22; 1 Chronicles 15:29

The witch of Endor – 1 Samuel 28

David's wives – 2 Samuel 3:2-5; 1 Chronicles 3:1-9

Tamar (David's daughter) – 2 Samuel 13:1-22

Abishag – 1 Kings 1:14; 2:13-25

Queen of Sheba – 1 Kings 10:1-13; 2 Chronicles 9:1-9

Widow of Zarephath – 1 Kings 17:8-24

Starving widow (Elisha) – 2 Kings 4:1-7

Shunammite woman – 2 Kings 4:8-37; 8:1-6

Naaman's wife's maid – 2 Kings 5:1-4

Athaliah – 2 Kings 11; 2 Chronicles 22:10-23:21

Pagan wives of Ezra's time – Ezra 10:18-44

Job's wife – Job 2:8-10

Proverbs 31 woman – Proverbs 31

Shulamite – Song of Solomon

Gomer – Hosea 1; 3

Jairus' daughter – Matthew 9:18-25; Mark 5:21-43; Luke 8:40-56

Woman w/blood flow – Matthew 9:20-22; Mark 5:25-34; Luke 8:43-48

Salome – Matthew 14:1-12; Mark 6:14-29

Peter's mother-in-law – Mark 1:29-31

Generous widow – Mark 12:41-44

Widow of Nain – Luke 7:11-17

Servant girl – Matthew 26:69-75; Mark 14:66-72; Luke 22:54-62; John 18:15-18, 25-26

Samaritan Woman – John 4:1-26, 39-43

Adultress – John 8:1-12

Sapphira – Acts 5:1-11

Rhoda – Acts 12:5-17

Lydia – Acts 16:11-15

Fortune teller – Acts 16:16-24

Bernice – Acts 25:13

Phoebe – Romans 16:1-2

Paul's supporters – Romans 16:3-15

Euodia & Syntyche – Philippians 4:2-3

Lois & Eunice – 2 Timothy 1:3-7

Elect lady – 2 John 1-3

Made in the USA
Middletown, DE
07 September 2024